No More Taking Away Recess and Other Problematic Discipline Practices

Dear Readers,

Much like the diet phenomenon *Eat This, Not That*, this series aims to replace some existing practices with approaches that are more effective—healthier, if you will—for our students. We hope to draw attention to practices that have little support in research or professional wisdom and offer alternatives that have greater support. Each text is collaboratively written by authors representing research and practice. Section 1 offers a practitioner's perspective on a practice in need of replacing and helps us understand the challenges, temptations, and misunderstandings that have led us to this ineffective approach. Section 2 provides a researcher's perspective on the lack of research to support the ineffective practice(s) and reviews research supporting better approaches. In Section 3, the author representing a practitioner's perspective gives detailed descriptions of how to implement these better practices. By the end of each book, you will understand both what not to do, and what to do, to improve student learning.

It takes courage to question one's own practice—to shift away from what you may have seen throughout your years in education and toward something new that you may have seen few if any colleagues use. We applaud you for demonstrating that courage and wish you the very best in your journey from this to that.

Best wishes,
—*Ellin Oliver Keene and Nell K. Duke, series editors*

No More Taking Away Recess and Other Problematic Discipline Practices

GIANNA CASSETTA

BROOK SAWYER

HEINEMANN
Portsmouth, NH

Heinemann
361 Hanover Street
Portsmouth, NH 03801–3912
www.heinemann.com

Offices and agents throughout the world

Cataloging-in-Publication Data is on file at the Library of Congress.
ISBN: 978-0-325-05114-7

Series editors: Ellin Oliver Keene and Nell K. Duke
Acquisitions editor: Margaret LaRaia
Production: Vicki Kasabian
Cover design: Lisa A. Fowler
Cover photograph: Photodisc/Getty Images/Andrew Ward/Life File/HIP
Interior design: Suzanne Heiser
Typesetting: Valerie Levy, Drawing Board Studios
Manufacturing: Veronica Bennett

Printed in the United States of America on acid-free paper
17 16 15 14 13 VP 1 2 3 4 5

CONTENTS

INTRODUCTION

ELLIN OLIVER KEENE

"When are we going to learn about classroom management?" In my nine years teaching education courses for teacher candidates at the University of Denver, this question was asked more than any other. Because I believed that classroom community was something a teacher refined through years of practice, I told my students that the best way to learn management practices was "on the ground"—in their internship and student teaching experiences. It wasn't a helpful response but it reflected the truth of my own classroom. I never used a particular approach; I relied on instinct and it usually worked . . . usually!

Across the country, teachers are dropping worksheets into the recycling bin, moving desks from rows into groups, and giving students daily structured time to do authentic work. But discipline practices haven't followed suit. For too long, discipline practices have been separate and disconnected from instruction. We might be following progressive models of content instruction, but when students misbehave we default to the way *we* were taught: systems of compliance, doling out punishment or reward. In the words of Daniel Pink, "autonomy leads to engagement" (2009, 110). If we want students to be engaged learners, they need to be self-directed ones. We know that choice, inquiry, and collaboration are critical elements of instruction, but in order for students to participate productively, we must create predictable, relationship-driven classrooms where students *learn* to assume responsibility for their behavior and interactions. This book shows the way.

Gianna Cassetta, a school leader, instructional coach, and former teacher, has worked in urban schools across the country, and Brook

Sawyer, a teacher educator and researcher, has conducted many studies that examined the ways in which adults' interactions and relationships with children shape their development, connected behavior to instruction, and showed us how to foster positive relationships with every student, even in difficult situations. As Brook explains in Section 2, "Your relationship with students also affects how you perceive the students' academic ability (Hughes, Gleason, and Zhang 2005), which in turn influences the instructional support you offer." Students need us to demonstrate effective social behavior implicitly, through the respect we show to them as individuals, but they also need explicit instruction on how to become more thoughtful, kind individuals and the space to practice these behaviors through peer collaboration, talk, choice.

You're reading this book because you want your classroom to be a joyful, productive place for you and your students. Gianna and Brook remind us that we don't have to be perfect, that maintaining any relationship over time isn't easy. We can't control what happens, but we *can* control how we respond to it. Regardless of the experiences students bring into the classroom, Gianna and Brook give us specific tools to prevent most difficulties and to solve the unavoidable ones.

NOT THIS

More Than Temporary Compliance, We Want Thoughtful, Independent Children

GIANNA CASSETTA

*The big question is whether you are going to be able
to say a hearty yes to your adventure.*
—Joseph Campbell

I was like you might be. I struggled with classroom management.

There I was, twenty years ago, in East Harlem, New York City, standing in front of a class of thirty-six fifth and sixth graders. I was supposed to do impossible things like get them from their tables to a carpeted meeting area where I would teach the whole class, and then back to tables where I would confer with individual students or teach in small groups while the rest of the class worked productively. Ha!

I had Hubba, a sixth grader who read on a first-grade level, and Erik, an angry child who had been passed from foster home to foster home, who threatened me with bodily harm just about every day; Dakar and Shakar, Rainey and Raya, two sets of twins who played identity tricks on me; Michelle, who let me know that if things didn't shape up her mother would sue me; Michael, whose body was too big and too tall for any of the furniture I was given; and then there was a group of fifth graders who had come from the star teacher. They reminded me repeatedly that I wasn't her. I told you; I struggled. Now you have a clearer picture of the details.

Like you, I was not born understanding how to differentiate for behavior or knowing which student behaviors are developmentally appropriate. And, unfortunately, I didn't gain any of that understanding or knowledge from graduate school or student teaching. My school had no system for classroom management. There was no rule book explaining that if X happens, do Y. The only rule was don't send children to the office. So . . . of course, I made decisions that were not very good for the esteem of some of my students. I made some decisions I am not proud of.

Back then, I was doing my best with what I knew how to do.

But there is a happy ending to my story, as I am sure there will be to yours if you struggle too. I dug my heels in; I don't get discouraged very easily. I let myself fall in love with my students, and for the most part, that came easily. I listened to the very wise advice of fellow educators who had figured it out years before me. I became a better teacher, better for myself and, more importantly, better for students. Children need adults to be better, so I gave my adventure a hearty "Yes." You can, too.

> **You'll learn the how and why in Sections 2 and 3, but first, let's spend some time exploring what happens when we rely on faulty discipline models.**

Scene from a Classroom: The Chaos of Rewards and Consequences

"Come to the carpet for reading instruction" seems like a simple direction, but the clamor of chairs, some being pushed under desks, some shoved astray, and the small confrontations—"Watch it!" "You pushed me!" "What's your problem?"—punctuating twenty-six students' movement to the carpet suggest otherwise. Mr. Ryan's back is turned, as he flips through his chart tablet to find the correct chart and then works to focus the text he has placed on the projector. Close to five minutes after the transition has been given, four students still haven't moved from their desks, and only a small fraction of the class have settled themselves on the carpet. The rest are still standing, or expressing annoyance with each other, or playing hand games to pass the time. As the volume in the classroom continues to escalate, Mr. Ryan finally notes the commotion. "This is not okay," he says as he turns toward them and shouts over the students' voices. "We are working really hard to win a pizza party. But you just lost 2 points for that." He moves to the dry erase board where the words *Pizza Party* are written with a row of tally marks beneath them, and he erases two tally marks. The students respond with a loud moan of "Aww!"

"This is your time you are wasting . . . let's see if we can get ready quickly and earn those points back." The students begin to settle and get quiet, but two remain at their desks talking. "Jordan and Eddie, you are over here on the carpet now or I am calling home!"

When we think about a well-managed classroom, this scene probably isn't one that comes to mind. Unfortunately though, many of us have struggled through similar situations ourselves, or have seen colleagues do so. When we don't have a clear vision for classroom management, when the techniques we are using are not embedded in a larger approach, when we are struggling, it is so natural, so tempting, to rely on rewards and consequences as a classroom management strategy.

Rewards and consequences are really two sides of the same coin. On one side, we are asking the child to comply because something good will happen if they do. On the other side, we are asking a child to comply because something bad will happen if they don't. The reality is that rewards and consequences only bring temporary compliance at best. Human beings, even young ones, just aren't that easy to control.

"What is so wrong with writing names on the board if it gets them to do what I want?" a struggling teacher earnestly asked me with tears in her eyes. In response, I focused on getting her to realize that it wasn't really getting her what she wanted. "Because this isn't that kind of school," I answered. "At this school, we teach students how to behave, we don't humiliate them into it. You don't want them to do what you tell them to because they are embarrassed or scared. You want them to make good choices because they have the skills to make them."

I wish that instead I had asked her, "What do you want, and why do you want it?" I wish I had explored the conflict instead of pretending she could move past it with a few words of wisdom, because that doesn't resolve anything. If I had asked her to imagine herself in a rewards and consequences system as an adult, she probably would have understood and been able to change her discipline practice sooner.

Imagine you're at a staff meeting, where there is a dry erase board with the name of each staff member and varying amounts of checks or X's next to the names. The principal notices you whispering with a colleague, walks over to the dry erase board, erases two checks by your name and says, "If you continue to talk during this staff meeting I will erase all of your check marks. If you want that pizza party, you'd better get your act together. Alice, Van, you are paying attention—I'm giving you two more checks each!" Humiliating? Absurd? Does it make you wonder how children feel when we do it to them?

There are certainly alternatives to the classroom scenario we just looked at. One approach being employed by some of the "high-performing" public schools in our country is called a "no excuses" approach. *No excuses* is a term that means that educators do not accept that the countless problems that have plagued public education can be accepted as excuses for why children do not succeed. Let's take a look at a classroom in a no excuses school.

Scene from a Classroom: No Excuses

Thirty-four students sit at individual desks arranged in rows facing the "front" of a classroom. The room is wallpapered with student work—there is a wall of science tests, math tests, reading tests. Big red numbers reading 90 percent or above label each paper. Slogans run along the top of the wall: "All of us WILL learn." "Climb the mountain to college." "Results matter."

Students are neatly dressed in khaki trousers, dark green polo shirts, and black shoes. The class is absolutely silent, as they wait for their third-period teacher to transition into their classroom. Ms. Daniels arrives, pushing her cart of teaching materials into the room. Mr. Hayden, the first- and second-period language arts teacher, says to Ms. Daniels, out loud for the class to hear, "Our scholars were awesome today. They worked hard, they focused on results. Not a single demerit." And then, turning his head toward the class, he adds emphatically, "I *expect* and I *trust* that this behavior will continue in science." Mr. Hayden rolls his cart out of the room and makes his way to meet his next class.

In this school, demerits are issued to students whenever they do not meet stated expectations. They are tracked on a daily basis. When individual students or the class as a whole receives what is determined to be an excessive number of demerits, they are subject to specific consequences ranging from loss of recess to Saturday detention to suspension.

Ms. Daniels turns to face the class, ready to begin teaching, and says, "Good morning, scholars." This is a prompt for the class to stand and in unison, respond, "Good morning, Ms. Daniels," to which she responds, "You may sit." She continues in a stern voice, "I want to remind you that the class got six demerits in science class yesterday. That is completely unacceptable. That is not what scholars at our school do. So get serious, get focused, and act like the scholars that you are!"

Ms. Daniels pauses for a moment, making eye contact with each student in the class. It is quiet enough to hear a pin drop. "Today I am expecting to see SLANT behaviors throughout the entire class period. Let's be sure they are clear in our heads. Get your minds and your bodies ready to say the SLANT chant!"

For ideas on how to create effective, valuable classroom rules and procedures,

see Section 2, page 33

Students instantly look more alert and upright, and every set of eyes pivots to the SLANT chart that reads:

- **S**it up.
- **L**ean in and listen.
- **A**nswer questions like a scholar.
- **N**od your head to show understanding.
- **T**rack the speaker.

Ms. Daniels begins with, "Give me an *S!*"

What Do You Want, and Why Do You Want It?

Many people, educators and noneducators alike, would read this scene and believe they were reading about a school where great classroom management happens. They would talk about the importance of rules and consequences in urban education, the necessity of high expectations, how we have to stop making excuses for student failure. They might appreciate the vision of college offered to students. Some would recognize the communication between teachers and the consistency in their messages. Some would appreciate the celebration of high grades.

Some might name instructional moves that communicate very explicit expectations, moves that stop impulsive behavior, reinforce desired behavior, and celebrate student success. For example, Mr. Hayden reinforces students' hard work and focus. Ms. Daniels reprimands students for the previous day's behavior, reminds them of the consequences, and then gives explicit reminders of expectations through the SLANT chart and chant. In a time where high-stakes tests are a priority, such scenes are often celebrated by politicians and the media for a high-expectations, no excuses approach to instruction. But I challenge every one of those people to look more deeply at this scene and to question the purpose and value of such instruction. I would ask, "If you applied these same techniques to an adult environment, would you not think this was also humiliating or absurd? What do we really want from children, and why do we want it?"

Think into the future, twenty years from now. Imagine you are in line at a coffee shop and you realize one of your former students is behind you. He's with his wife and two children, who are four and seven years old. He asks you to sit down with them to catch up, and you, of course, are thrilled. Imagine that interaction. What social skills would you hope your former student demonstrates in this interaction with you, his wife, his two children? Jot those down. Then, rank those social skills in order of importance.

Social Skill	Rank

In Section 2, you will learn about the five competencies of social and emotional learning, and the research behind why they are important: self-awareness, self-management (impulse control), social awareness (understanding of others), relationship skills, and decision-making (problem-solving) skills. Were any of these or related terms on your list of social skills you hoped your former student would demonstrate? Now, reread the scene in the fifth-grade no excuses classroom and examine if any of the five competencies of social and emotional learning were being taught.

In the no excuses fifth-grade classroom you read about, teachers were imposing their own values on students regarding student behavior ("That is not what scholars at our school do"), but never asking

How does self-control and awareness of behavior relate to academic performance? Learn the research about how they're connected

see Section 2, page 20

students to self-assess. In fact, it would be difficult for students to self-assess against such unspecific feedback. What does it mean to be "awesome"? What exact behaviors did they display to earn such a compliment? These specifics would be important for students to know, so that they could, if they were self-aware, replicate them. One might argue that students were learning impulse control. But in order for impulse control to be a skill, one must be able to manage impulses independently. In this scenario, the adults were managing student impulses through consequences and accolades. Students were required to hear the perspectives of teachers but were not asked to consider their own. There was no opportunity for forming relationships in a classroom setting where students don't move except at the teacher's direction to perform a greeting or a chant. And all decisions in such a setting appeared to be made by the teacher.

Both children and adults learn social behaviors in every situation and setting. So if students were not learning the five competencies of social and emotional learning in this particular classroom setting, what were they learning?

Classroom Management and Control Are Not Synonymous

Control leads to compliance; autonomy leads to engagement.
—Daniel Pink

In trying to determine a widely accepted definition of classroom management, I found the task nearly impossible. But there were recurring themes. Among them were classroom discipline, an orderly environment, an environment that supports student learning, an environment where learning can occur despite disruptions, and an environment that enhances social and moral growth.

With such varied and vague definitions, it is no wonder that classroom management is noted as a leading cause of teacher burnout. There is little work done to prepare teachers for thoughtfully and effectively managing a classroom. Schools often lack their own training or don't even offer schoolwide approaches to support teachers. This makes it very tempting for teachers to institute practices that get short-term but quick results, such as the no excuses example you read, or the more widespread practice of using rewards and consequences—the marble jar, the pizza party, the lost recess, the name on the chalkboard, the tally points, the threats of calls home.

In order to really explore classroom management, we need to proceed with a shared definition. In my twenty years as an educator, I have worked through various philosophical approaches to classroom management like the ones we have already explored, and, with lots of experimenting under my belt, I've had time to come to what I believe is a necessarily complex definition of classroom management, which I will define in the next section.

What We Pay Attention to Tells Us Who We Are

When teachers ask me, "How do I fix my classroom management?," my answer is usually along the lines of "I hope you are ready for a long, hard answer—this is complicated work, and there are no quick fixes." As I see it, classroom management is a result of the intersection between any given teachers':

1. values/beliefs
2. knowledge of child development
3. design and implementation of classroom systems
4. communication of expectations
5. teaching skill
6. relationships with students

Essayist and philosopher José Ortega y Gasset said, "Tell me what you pay attention to and I will tell you who you are" (1958, 94). The values that you may not even know you carry within you manifest themselves through what you pay attention to in a classroom setting. They influence your relationships with students; they impact delivery of instruction; they guide classroom environment, expectations, rewards, consequences. Because of the reach of influence your values have, it is important to explore them and name them. At times, it is important to question them and even to leave them at home.

Let's compare how two different fifth-grade teachers view their work. The juxtaposition of these two teachers' perspectives is intended as a tool for you to think about what beliefs, whether consciously or unconsciously, are reflected in your classroom management approach.

Fifth-Grade Teacher 1: "Because I believe learning should be about respect for rules and academic achievement, child development is not a primary concern."

"I know from experience fifth graders can listen well and work for sustained periods of time. I have learned that around issues of fairness, arguments can erupt and escalate. My classroom is designed to limit interactions and the possibility of eruptions. Students sit in assigned seats at all times, at desks arranged in rows facing the teacher. Materials are all stored in desks. Student talk happens with my permission, one student at a time, as a result of raising hands and being called on. Student movement and material management is kept to a minimum. There are long, sustained periods of silent work. Classroom rules and behavioral expectations are created by me and are clearly stated, publicly posted, and routinely revisited. Consequences for rule-breaking behavior follow a 'progressive discipline system' (for example, warning, phone call home, detention, parent conference). Consequences are public, swift, and consistent.

Students who follow rules are rewarded (i.e., Friday afternoon trip to fast-food vendor, points that can be cashed in for a prize). Arguing is not tolerated, nor is discussion around fairness. My teaching follows a standards map and is delivered through a direct instructional approach. Cold calling is often employed to keep students attentive. There is always a written product, often in the form of an exit ticket, for assessment. I meet with students before or after school, sometimes to deliver consequences (detention, for example) or for tutoring. I often speak with children at home to help with homework. I keep in close contact with parents so they understand behavioral or academic concerns."

Fifth-Grade Teacher 2: "Because I believe in autonomy, social development, and academic achievement . . ."

"I made sure to research fifth-grade development specifically, in order to inform decisions I make about classroom management and how to build autonomy and engagement. I know fifth graders have a growing awareness around issues of fairness and seek to explore what is right or wrong. I know they need to talk in order to think—best thinking happens when they process out loud. My classroom is designed for movement between whole-class, small-group, and individual work. There is a whole-class meeting area with a carpet and benches to provide choices to accommodate growing bodies. Workspaces are at shared tables, and materials are stored in packs that hang off of the backs of rocking chairs to allow for some continuous movement. There are also floor pillows and a couch to provide additional independent work space.

(continues)

(continued)

"The schedule allows for multiple transitions between independent and group work, and two social breaks are built into the classroom schedule. Classroom rules have been created with the class and are posted and referred to often. Students are often reminded of expectations and are praised highly when expectations are met. Specific praise far exceeds reminders. Consequences are connected to the rule-breaking behavior—for example, rough play at recess means sitting out of recess. Roughhousing in the classroom results in a break in a buddy teacher's classroom. Students who struggle to meet behavioral expectations often have individual conferences with the teacher where an individualized action plan is set. Students are taught conversation skills for discussing disagreements, and the issue of fairness is built into many read-alouds and class discussions.

"My teaching considers the standards but is also differentiated to meet the academic needs and student interests within the class. I use a variety of talk structures—partner, small group, whole class, and occasionally, cold calling—to hear a variety of voices and inputs. I carefully listen to and take notes on students during the lesson as a means of assessing student learning. There are varying degrees of student choice built into every lesson and student-led reflection on their own performance. I hold a daily morning meeting to get to know each student personally and for the class to know each other. I often share personal stories in the classroom and invite students to do the same. I eat lunch with and play with my students at recess and keep in close contact with parents so I can get to know students through their eyes."

In these two examples, you can see that classroom management isn't isolated from anything else you do when you teach, but a manifestation of what you believe as a teacher. Both teachers have strengths, but they use them very differently based on their beliefs.

There are times when classroom management choices are informed by far more sinister beliefs, such as the belief that children aren't capable of making good choices for themselves. But if you are reading this book, you must believe children can be taught to make good decisions. It is important to understand the reasons children misbehave in order to support them with effective classroom management. We will explore those reasons in Section 3.

For developmental and situational reasons for misbehavior

see Section 3, page 50

When we provide a safe, joyful, productive learning environment where students develop the ability to self-regulate, show empathy, solve problems, have a confident sense of self, and cultivate relationships, we have effective classroom management. Moving forward in this book, when I talk about classroom management, that is what I am talking about.

WHY NOT? WHAT WORKS?

Relationships and Good Instruction Are the Foundation of Classroom Management

BROOK SAWYER

As Gianna explained in Section 1, there is more to managing a classroom than meets the eye. It may be clear that in classrooms that are chaotic and/or disordered, like Mr. Ryan's classroom, children have fewer opportunities to learn either academic or social skills. However, what may be less obvious is that a teacher, such as Ms. Daniels, who appears to have a well-managed classroom may in fact be using practices that are not beneficial to students' development and learning. In excessively rigid classrooms like Ms. Daniels', students have few opportunities to develop advanced social skills through interaction with peers and the teacher. And yet, knowing that the U.S. Department of Education (2005) cites that almost half (42 percent) of teachers report that "student misbehavior interferes with my teaching," we understand how that rigidity happens. If you are experiencing frustration with classroom management, know that you are not alone . . . and know that things can improve! This section will explain the research on why children's social and emotional abilities are important to their academic success, the role of a caring social environment in classroom management, and practices that create an effective learning environment.

Neither a Disciplinarian nor a Goody Dispenser: Why Rewards and Consequences Don't Work

In my early experience as a middle school teacher, I tried many of the short-term approaches that Gianna described in Section 1. The system of rewards and consequences felt "off" to me, but I wasn't sure why or how I could do things differently. It slowly began to dawn on me that classroom management is more than setting up rules, procedures, and consequences to "manage" student behavior; classroom management is about building relationships with students and teaching social skills along with academic skills. Let's explore some common discipline strategies and why they don't work effectively.

"Taking Away" Doesn't Show Students How They Should Behave

For practices that give children skills to grow socially and emotionally

see Section 3, page 64

In a study of more than one hundred elementary school teachers, Moberly and her colleagues (2005) found that the most common consequence for student misbehavior was taking away students' recess time. Taking away recess is problematic because physical activity supports brain development and improves children's engagement in learning (e.g., concentration) and behavior (Ratey 2008). Mahar and colleagues (2006) found that elementary school children who are frequently off task improved their on-task behavior by 20 percent when they engaged in regular physical activity at school. In particular, when students with ADHD exercised regularly, teachers reported that the students learned better and exhibited less problem behavior (Verret et al. 2009). Taken together, this means that the students who are the most likely to lose recess are the kids who most need recess!

Public reprimands or punishments that cause students to feel embarrassment, anger, or other similarly negative emotions do not work (Landrum and Kauffman 2006; Woolfolk Hoy and Weinstein 2006). Often when teachers reprimand students, the best-case scenario is that students make no change in their behavior (Leinhardt, Weidman, and Hammond 1987), and the worst-case scenario is that students actually increase their negative behaviors (Van Acker, Grant, and Henry 1996). Punishing students does not provide students with a positive model of how they should behave (Landrum and Kauffman 2006). Students learn that their behavior was ineffective but they may not know what they should have done instead.

Rewards for Expected Behaviors Don't Foster Independence

Many teachers believe that providing a pizza party or adding marbles to a jar for good behavior is a different strategy than taking away recess for bad behavior. However, both systems often rely on the "If you do this, I'll give you (or take away) that" strategy. In this way, these strategies attempt to control how the students act, draw students' focus away from the act of learning toward the expected reward or punishment, and do not support children's internal motivation to be independent learners (Reeve 2006). For example, if students know they will earn a raffle ticket when they complete their book project, their goal may be to finish as quickly as possible rather than to engage fully in the process. They are not doing the behavior for the right reasons. Additionally, when we interfere with students learning how to control their own behavior, we make them less likely to display competent behavior in other situations or when the reward is no longer available (Elias and Schwab 2006; Reeve 2006).

Are rewards always bad? Definitely not! There are appropriate ways to use them. At the end of this section, we'll explore how to help individual students who struggle even after we have put various evidence-based strategies in place. The "trick" is that rewards or reinforcers are used to give students feedback about their behavior (rather than control their behavior) and should be implemented in a carefully systematic way.

I must make one clarifying point about giving students rewards. Sometimes as teachers we want to treat our children to stickers, pencils, pizza parties, and so on as a way to demonstrate affection. That is okay! Researchers call this *noncontingent reinforcement*, which means that students don't need to perform in any certain way to earn this reward. This type of strategy won't harm students' development of internal motivation (Reeve 2006).

A System of Rewards and Consequences Takes More Work and Accomplishes Less

One very practical reason to avoid a rewards and consequences classroom management system is that it is a lot of work. You will find yourself working harder to accomplish less than you will with the alternative practices we propose in this book. Because you, and not your students, are in control of their behavior, you have to constantly monitor and intervene (Elias and Schwab 2006). For example, you plan to differentiate learning using teacher-led small-group work but instead spend your time putting out fires (or having to give out raffle tickets to keep students on task) rather than attending to the small group that needs your instruction. This results in a considerable loss of instructional time.

Although a rewards and consequences system can feel unpleasant for us as teachers, sometimes we take on this role because we believe it's best for our students. In truth, it isn't. Your students may behave for you in your tightly controlled classroom, but what happens when you have a substitute teacher or, more importantly, when they're on their own? You have created a system where they are overly dependent on you and when you're not there, your students will be at a loss for what to do. You don't want that. You want them to know they have the tools to navigate challenges on their own.

Positive, Self-Directed Behavior Needs to Be Taught

We need to remind ourselves that when a child misbehaves, it is not only uncomfortable for us but also uncomfortable for that child. No one enjoys dwelling in negative emotions. Just as we know that students don't enter our classrooms having mastered all of the academic standards, students also require our assistance in becoming socially and emotionally competent. (And let's face it, as adults, we still struggle at times with these skills.)

In an evaluation of school programs that taught social and emotional skills, students who were explicitly taught social and emotional skills in school demonstrated more positive attitudes and behavior (and fewer instances of misbehavior) than students who had not (Durlak et al. 2011). These social and emotional skills emerge from the fundamental needs that all humans, children and adults, share: relatedness, autonomy, and competence. If these needs are met in our classroom, then children have the necessary foundation to be successful in school and beyond. Based on these needs, Payton et al. (2008) identified five social and emotional skills that teachers can help students develop. **Self-awareness** allows them to identify their own emotions. **Self-management** includes how students control their impulses, display their feelings appropriately, and set and achieve goals for themselves. **Social awareness** is the ability to take the perspective of others and display empathy. **Positive relationship skills** allow them to develop friendships with peers

> To see what these positive behaviors can look like in the classroom
>
> see Section 3, page 49

and close relationships with teachers and other adults. Students also need to be **responsible decision makers** in regard to safety, respectful treatment of people, and academic learning. These abilities work together and should not be thought of as discrete and isolated skills. For example, Javier can identify that he is angry when he doesn't get to work with his friend Dominick during the science activity (self-awareness). Knowing he is angry may help him control his impulses so that he doesn't speak harshly to his teacher or rip his paper in anger (self-management). He also realizes that it will hurt Jessica's, his current partner, feelings if he complains that he doesn't want to work with her (social awareness). He smiles at Jessica as they move to their assigned area of the room and begin work on their project (positive relationship skills and responsible decision making).

You may have noticed that the language used to describe Javier's successful navigation of his emotions is *awareness* and *management*. These words communicate the value of being conscious and in control of one's emotions, able to reflect before reacting. Although children may learn these abilities at home, they also need to be taught by the classroom teacher so children know how to apply these skills in different contexts.

Evaluate Your Classroom Management System

Now that you know what the social and emotional skills are and why a rewards and consequences system doesn't work to teach them, take a moment to ask yourself some questions about your current classroom management system. Use these questions as a reminder and rationale for effective classroom management. (See Figure 2–1.) As you continue to read this section and Section 3, you'll learn specific practices that will help you answer *yes* to each of these questions. You might find that you can answer *yes* to some, but not to all of them. If so, then you'll have a good sense of what to focus on as you continue reading.

How Are Social Skills Linked with Academic Performance?

In this world of high-stakes testing, we may feel that focusing on teaching these skills is a luxury—that all our time has to be spent on academics. Yet, the reality is that students who are able to interact and engage in socially and emotionally appropriate ways perform better in school (e.g., Caprara et al. 2000; Valiente et al. 2008; Wentzel

Figure 2–1 Questions to Evaluate Classroom Management Practice

Questions You Can Use to Evaluate Your Classroom Management Practice
• Does this system allow for my students to feel connected to their peers and me (relatedness) or will it create a "me versus them" situation?
• Does this system allow for my students to make independent choices (autonomy) or does it serve to control children's behavior?
• Does this system allow for my students to reflect on their behavior to identify what they did well and what they need to improve upon (competence) or am I the one who is telling them what they did well/ not well?

1993). Children who are socially and emotionally competent are more focused in their learning due to their abilities to demonstrate self-control, pay attention, and persist in completing tasks (e.g., Coolahan et al. 2000; Normandeau and Guay 1998; Wentzel 1993). These behaviors lead to better academic performance (e.g., Graziano et al. 2007; Hughes et al. 2008).

Children Need to Feel Part of Their School and Classroom Community

Classrooms are learning communities. In classroom communities, the teacher and students have "shared experiences, shared goals, and shared responsibility" (Watson and Battistich 2006, 266). In such a community, the student feels connected to the teacher and classmates

For ideas on how to foster community

see Section 3, page 68

(relatedness), is supported to meet advanced learning objectives successfully (competence), and has confidence to engage in learning independently (autonomy). We create classroom communities by providing opportunities for students to work together and communicate their learning with their peers as well as involving students in setting classroom goals and sharing decision making, such as developing the rules and collectively brainstorming as a class when problems arise (Watson and Battistich 2006). Students who are part of positive school and classroom communities perform better socially and academically (e.g., Patrick et al. 2003; Watson and Battistich 2006). They do so because they care about keeping their community a positive place to be, not because they are working toward a reward or avoiding a consequence (Solomon et al. 2000). And these effects can be long term: when students experience being part of a community in the elementary grades, they have better social adjustment in middle school (Battistich, Schaps, and Wilson 2004) and are less likely to drop out of high school and thus limit their employment opportunities (Wehlage et al. 1989).

The relationships you form with individual students set the stage for how students treat one another and whether a caring community is formed. In fact, harsh punishment may lead classmates to relate more strongly with the disciplined student than with you (Woolfolk Hoy and Weinstein 2006). The opposite also may happen. Your reaction to a child who struggles to behave may lead your students to think there is something not worthy about that classmate, leading their peers to reject them (White, Jones, and Sherman 1998), which results in diminished feelings of competence and relatedness for the struggling student. Another point is when consequences are given to some students and not others, students perceive the teacher as being unfair (Woolfolk Hoy and Weinstein 2006).

A Positive Teacher–Student Relationship Is Necessary for Academic Success. Community begins with each individual child's relationship to the teacher. Researchers consistently find that when students have positive relationships with teachers, they behave better, are more engaged in learning, and do better academically (Birch and Ladd 1997; Cornelius-White 2007; Elias and Haynes 2008; Graziano et al. 2007; Hughes et al. 2008; Ladd, Birch, and Buhs 1999;

Larsen, Wanless, and Rimm-Kaufman, manuscript under revision; Skinner, Wellborn, and Connell 1990; Valiente et al. 2008). Your relationship with students also affects how you perceive the students' academic ability (Hughes, Gleason, and Zhang 2005), which in turn influences the instructional support you offer. Students, including those who have behavior disorders, report that their most effective teachers established caring relationships with them (Woolfolk Hoy and Weinstein 2006). See Figure 2–2 for the hallmark characteristics of three types of teacher–student relationships (Birch and Ladd 1997; Pianta 1999).

Think about a time when you tried something new. Didn't you do better when you had a positive supportive person there to encourage and help you? A close relationship with a teacher affords children feelings of emotional security that allow them to safely explore and engage in the learning environment, while conflictual or dependent relationships interfere with children's engagement in learning (main idea of the extended attachment theory; e.g., Birch and Ladd 1997; Pianta 1999). As the teacher, you provide encouraging and affirming support, differentiate learning appropriately because of your in-depth knowledge of the child, scaffold instruction to help the child meet the demands of the situation, and so on.

For an example of how to support students through academic frustrations

see Section 3, page 52

In a conflictual relationship, the teacher may offer the student less challenging tasks, leading the child to think the teacher doubts the child's abilities *or* the teacher may interact less with the student and thus provide less of the needed instructional support for the child to succeed (which makes it less likely the student tries something challenging in the future). In a dependent relationship, the student lacks confidence in his ability and believes he can't accomplish the learning task without continual reassurance and assistance from the teacher. Thus, this student won't take the risk to try challenging activities, which can limit his academic development.

Figure 2–2 Types of Teacher–Student Relationships

Type of Teacher–Student Relationship	What It Looks Like
Close (positive)	• Teacher displays an affectionate, sensitive, and responsive demeanor to students. • Teacher provides assistance, instructionally and emotionally, to help children achieve their goals. • Teacher knows student well (knows what child feels confident or anxious about in the classroom but also knows about child outside of school—e.g., whether the child has brothers/sisters, what the child likes to do on weekends). • Teacher and student enjoy spending time together.
Conflictual (negative)	• Teacher displays more frequent irritation at the student (e.g., when student misbehaves or is not prepared for the activity). • Teacher provides less instructional and emotional support. • Teacher may know less about the student than other students in the classroom. • Teacher and student are distant with one another.
Dependent (negative)	• Student overrelies on the teacher and does not independently participate in the learning environment of the classroom (e.g., student asks teacher for help on every math word problem).

What are the long-term effects of teacher–student relationships? If you've ever wondered if your relationships with children make a difference, the research shows they do. Your relationships with students still influence them when they are no longer in your classroom—even eight years later (e.g., Hamre and Pianta 2001; Hughes et al. 2008; Wu, Hughes, and Kwok 2010). For instance, second- and third-grade children who had positive teacher–child relationships outperformed children in negative relationships over the remainder of elementary school in terms of engagement and their achievement in math and reading (Wu, Hughes, and Kwok 2010). Sadly, early negative relationships with teachers contribute to later problems. Negative relationships between kindergarten students and their teachers were associated with more conduct problems in upper elementary school (grades 5–6) for all children and through middle school (grades 7–8) for boys; these negative relationships also predicted lower reading and math achievement in first through fourth grades (Hamre and Pianta 2001). Through our relationships, we communicate to students what we expect of them—good and bad—and this often becomes a self-fulfilling prophecy (Montague and Rinaldi 2001; Thompson 2004). We also may communicate these messages to other teachers in our school, with the result that children do not begin each school year with a clean slate. In fact, the development of positive relationships with children who display problem behaviors early in their schooling diminishes the frequency of problem behaviors in later grades (Hamre and Pianta 2001).

Positive Teacher–Student Relationships Are Essential but Not Always Easy. One important point to acknowledge is that relationships involve two people. The student's behavior affects how you interact with her as well as vice versa. Undoubtedly, it is easier to build a close relationship with Iman, who follows instructions most of the time and responds quickly to redirection if she is not following the rules, than with Emmanuel, who rarely follows directions despite numerous attempts to keep him on task. We as teachers have to be aware of how we interact with *all* of our students and what consequences, intended or unintended, our relationship with them has on their behavior and learning. Every teacher wants to build a positive relationship with every student we have. Yet despite our best intentions, research tells us that there are certain groups of children who are more or less likely to share a close relationship with us.

Teachers develop more positive relationships with children who are more mature and intelligent (Ladd, Birch, and Buhs 1999; Mantzicopoulos 2005). They develop more negative relationships with children who display regular problem behaviors, including anger and hyperactivity (Justice et al. 2008; Ladd, Birch, and Buhs 1999; Mantzicopoulos 2005; Thijs and Koomen 2009). On the surface, this makes perfect sense; it is easier to form positive relationships with students who are humming along in the daily life of the classroom. But let's dig deeper.

On average, girls share closer relationships with their teachers than boys (Birch and Ladd 1997; Hamre and Pianta 2001; O'Connor and McCartney 2006). Boys tend to have more difficulty adjusting to early elementary school and are more likely to display more challenging behaviors than girls (Ponitz et al. 2009). For instance, developmentally, they have more difficulty staying on task. As a result, they are more likely to be reprimanded by teachers and need behavioral interventions. It is important for us as teachers to recognize that these differences are typical and developmental—not that "boys are troublemakers."

For an example of typical and developmentally appropriate boy "misbehavior" and how to address it

see Section 3, page 56

Boys may require more explicit teaching of social skills than girls. Additionally, anger is more detrimental to the teacher–student relationship for boys than girls. Boys who displayed anger had more negative relationships with their teachers than girls who displayed anger (Justice et al. 2008). So an angry boy is highly unlikely to have a positive teacher–student relationship, unless the teacher is able to recognize that he requires additional support.

Children who are members of an ethnic-minority group and of low-socioeconomic status also are more likely to share negative relationships with their teachers (Hughes et al. 2005; Ladd et al. 1999; O'Connor and McCartney 2006). Sadly, in the United States, children from ethnic-minority groups disproportionately live in poverty— 65 percent of African American and Hispanic children live in poverty compared to 31 percent of white children (NCCP 2013). Students who are lower income or ethnic minority are referred to the office for discipline infractions more than their higher income or white peers (Doyle 2006; Gay 2006). Also, regardless of behavior, African American males were twice as likely as white males and black females and six times as likely as white females to be suspended (Gay 2006). As teachers, we must remember that children who live in poverty are more likely to be exposed to risk, such as exposure to violence and harsher parenting, and these risk factors influence their behavior in the classroom (Conroy and Brown 2004; Qi and Kaiser 2003).

Another distressing fact is that children who live in poverty perform alarmingly worse academically in school than children who are middle- or upper-socioeconomic status (Hoff 2013). However, research indicates that forming positive relationships with poor and ethnic-minority students supports their behavior and academics. A teacher who communicates caring and high academic expectations is especially important to students who are poor and ethnic minority; these students are more likely to feel alienated from the educational system and thus have greater need to develop trusting relationships with teachers (Gregory and Weinstein 2008; Katz 1999). In a study of African American elementary students who displayed problem behaviors in school, Decker, Dona, and Christenson (2007) found that having a more positive relationship with teachers was related to better behavior, fewer office referrals/suspensions, and higher academic performance. Watson and Battistich (2006) make a powerful statement about our roles as teachers: "Poor and minority students are least likely to experience their classrooms and schools as caring communities and the most likely to benefit when they do" (270).

One finding that may surprise you is that children who are shy or inhibited are less likely to develop close relationships with their teachers (Justice et al. 2008; Thijs and Koomen 2009). This may be explained by the fact that shy children interact less with their teachers than children who are socially bold (Rimm-Kaufman et al. 2002). Thus, teachers most likely will need to put extra effort into getting to know the shy children in their classrooms.

We raise awareness of these patterns not to be critical of teachers, but rather in the hope that we can be more mindful of this tendency and extend ourselves to more students. It is only when we are aware that we can purposefully adjust our actions so that positive relationships can be developed that support children's success in school.

For specific behaviors to promote positive teacher–student relationships

see Section 3, page 68

Although some teachers may "believe that students need to earn their [teachers'] respect, relationship, concern and interest" (Woolfolk Hoy and Weinstein 2006, 209), a child can't meet that expectation without a guiding hand. A positive teacher–student relationship communicates "I care about you and believe you can succeed."

Provide Appropriate and Engaging Instruction

It probably comes as no surprise that when we provide instruction that is appropriate and engaging, students' behavior is better (Bohn, Roehrig, and Pressley 2004), even without using any rewards or reinforcers (Reeve 2006). When instruction is developmentally appropriate, teacher–student relationships are more positive as well (Mantzicopoulos 2005). In fact, students report that their most effective teachers make learning fun (Woolfolk Hoy and Weinstein 2006). Although it is beyond the scope of this section (or book) to cover the robust evidence on instructional practices, we wish to highlight several key strategies that influence student behavior: having high expectations of all learners, differentiating and scaffolding instruction, providing choice and relevant instruction, timing and pacing the lessons, and engaging students in cooperative learning.

High Academic Expectations with Differentiated, Scaffolded Instruction. Teachers must value the active participation and success of all students as well as communicate that value to their students (Epstein et al. 2008). In their study of "effective teachers," Bohn, Roehrig, and Pressley (2004) found that effective teachers held high academic expectations for all their students and ineffective teachers expressed doubt about some students' skills to do the work. When students have ample opportunities to actively engage with or respond to instruction (also called "opportunities to respond"), they do better academically, are more on task, and exhibit less problem behavior (Kern and Clemens 2007). Opportunities to respond may include using manipulatives to demonstrate an answer to a math problem, writing an answer to a teacher question on an individual whiteboard, or using sticky notes to take notes on their use of comprehension strategies during reading.

Having high expectations does not mean that you expect the same performance from every student on the same task. Students may misbehave when tasks are too difficult or too easy (Bohn, Roehrig, and Pressley 2004). To ensure that all students are performing at their appropriate level, we need to differentiate instruction (Gettinger and Kohler 2006). Students should be challenged but still able to experience success (Emmer, Evertson, and Anderson 1980). As children gain more competence, teachers scaffold instruction by providing less support than what is needed when they first attempt new learning (Pressley et al. 2003). Researchers have found that teachers provide misbehaving students with less instructional support than

> **For an example of high academic expectations with support**
>
> see Section 3, page 53

children who are behaving (Jones and Bouffard 2012). Yet, these are the students who most likely need the most support. The misbehavior may be due to an inappropriate level of instruction or task for that particular child. If students are misbehaving to avoid tasks that are appropriately challenging, one evidenced-based strategy to increase student participation and decrease misbehavior is "the interspersal of several easy and brief problems or tasks among other longer or more difficult tasks. For example, a single-digit multiplication problem may be interspersed after every third four-digit multiplication problem" (Kern and Clemens 2007, 69).

Engagement and Differentiation Through Choice and Relevant Instruction. One way to differentiate instruction is to provide opportunities for children to make choices. This leads to better academic and behavioral performance (Bohn, Roehrig, and Pressley 2004). Providing choice is a good way to connect children's interests and background knowledge to the instructional content (Emmer, Evertson, and Anderson 1980). Kern, Bambara, and Fogt (2002) provided a variety of choice opportunities to students with severe emotional and behavioral disorders and found that students became more engaged and exhibited less problem behavior. Choices were connected to interests of the students, and students were permitted to make choices about the activities they were to complete, the materials they could use (such as which books they would read), or the order of tasks they were to complete.

Teachers must also make learning relevant for students. Teachers should communicate the utility of what students are learning. To this end, instructional activities should be as authentic as possible (Pressley et al. 2003). For instance, writing instruction can be interdisciplinary where students are asked to write about their field trip to the nature preserve from the perspective of a scientist. Additionally, it is critical that instruction is culturally relevant (Gay 2006; Thompson 2004). Students should be "taught in ways that value and build on their culture" (Thompson 2004, 206). By creating opportunities to get to know your students better, teachers can make stronger connections between the curriculum and students' background knowledge. McIntyre and Turner (2013) provide a variety of recommendations of how to make these connections: (1) keep a journal of what you learn about students from having in-depth conversations with them and use this information to inform instruction, such as helping students select books on topics that interest them; (2) have students create artifacts, such as research projects or autobiographical books, about their lives or home countries; (3) use diverse instructional materials, such as hip-hop lyrics when teaching students critical reading and writing skills; and (4) invite family members to plan and participate in projects of interest with their children.

Plan Activities with Children's Attention Span in Mind. Effective teachers consider and monitor the attention span of their students (Emmer, Evertson, and Anderson 1980). The attention span of younger elementary students may only be ten to fifteen minutes (Epstein et al. 2008). For students of any age, switching activities frequently or incorporating movement into the lesson or between activities is a good way to support students' engagement. Incorporating a variety of activity structures in a variety of locations, such as whole group on the carpet, small group work at a back table, individual work at desks, is a way to sustain student attention (Epstein et al. 2008). Another "trick" is to schedule activities students greatly enjoy after challenging activities, such as scheduling math before special area times like physical education or art (Epstein et al. 2008).

Create Opportunities for Cooperative Learning. Cooperative groups or peer tutoring can be a good choice for many reasons. As students practice and enhance their social and emotional skills in these peer groups, they're likely to be more engaged, be more successful at learning, have less problem behavior, and develop a more positive classroom community (Johnson and Johnson 2004; Kamps et al. 1999; Solomon et al. 2000). Cooperative learning activities should be designed so students' learning is interdependent, not a task that one student in the group could feasibly complete on her own (Johnson and Johnson 2004; Pressley et al. 2003). The teacher can facilitate the development of social skills by explicitly teaching procedures and processes for engaging in group work, including teaching the group members how to assess how well they are accomplishing their goals.

Give Children Guidelines on How to Behave: Rules and Procedures

Although some teachers worry that enforcing rules will create a negative atmosphere in the classroom, it actually does just the opposite— as long as you are positive and respectful in your interactions with students. If you don't remind or redirect a student to remember the classroom rule to "use kind words" when he is teasing a classmate, the teased child feels abandoned and certainly not part of a caring community. In fact, students themselves, including students with severe behavior problems, report having greater respect for teachers who "exercise authority without being rigid, threatening or punitive" (Woolfolk Hoy and Weinstein 2006, 185). Through enforcing expectations, you maintain a caring community (Woolfolk Hoy and Weinstein 2006), and Gianna will share examples of how this works in Section 3. See Guidelines for Creating Classroom Rules, Figure 2–3.

Create Clear Procedures. Students feel more secure and behave better when they are familiar with the set of procedures and activities that happen during their day. First, having a clear and predictable schedule to your day is a way to increase positive behavior (Kern and Clemens 2007). Think how a "surprise event" (like having an unexpected team meeting or your teaching partner out sick) can really affect your mood and behavior on a day. This happens to children too. Second, having consistent procedures that children are taught to follow quickly ensures that you are not losing valuable instructional time to logistical details, such as how to enter and exit the classroom, how to retrieve and put away materials (e.g., books, scissors, math manipula-

Figure 2–3 Guidelines for Creating Classroom Rules

Guidelines for Creating Classroom Rules

1. ***Rules should be positive.*** In other words, rules should communicate to children what they should do, not what they shouldn't do (Bullara 1993; Jolivette and Steed 2010; Mayer 1995). For instance, "Use kind words" rather than "Do not be mean."

2. ***Rules should be few in number.*** Keep your number of classroom rules concise (Jolivette and Steed 2010). Why? Research indicates that for rules to be effective, they need to be referred to often during the school day and consistently enforced (more on this will be discussed below). It is not reasonable to expect students or yourself to remember a lengthy list of rules. Kern and Clemens (2007) suggest a maximum of five rules.

3. ***Rules should be posted.*** By posting classroom rules, you have a visual way to remind students of the rules (Gettinger and Kohler 2006; Mayer 1995). Make sure you post them in an area of the room that children can easily see, including posting them at students' eye level.

Who should create the rules? A common question is who should create the classroom rules—the school, the teacher, the teacher with the students? There is no consensus in research to indicate if one way is better than another (Carter and Doyle 2006). Some researchers recommend forming rules with students because when students have a say in the classroom rules, they are more invested (or have greater "buy-in") and thus may be more likely to follow the rules (Elias and Schwab 2006; Mayer 1995; Solomon et al. 2000).

tives), how to turn in assignments, and what students should do when they need help during independent work (Sprick 2009; Epstein et al. 2008). It is important to make procedures simple and efficient (Leinhardt, Weidman, and Hammond 1987). Predictable rules, procedures and schedules also are very helpful for children who are English language learners (Tabors 2008), allowing them to connect new words to consistent actions and objects.

One critical procedure to consider carefully is how to handle transition time between activities. Does it surprise you to know that transitions make up approximately 25 percent of your school day (Epstein et al. 2008)?! Transitions are complex in that students often are required to do a number of tasks in a short amount of time (Leinhardt, Weidman, and Hammond 1987). They need to complete the demands of the current task as well as prepare for the future task; for instance, they may have two minutes to put away their math books and manipulatives, push in their chairs, and quietly move to the carpet with their language arts books and pencil. Remember Mr. Ryan from Section 1 and the chaos that ensued because he was preparing for the next lesson rather than focusing on guiding students through the transition? During transition times, it is vital that teachers monitor students' actions, so it is crucial that you prepare in advance for the next activity.

For guidelines on creating procedures

see Section 3, page 64

Provide Explicit Instruction on Rules and Procedures. As Gettinger and Kohler (2006) indicate, teachers should "approach the teaching of classroom rules as systematically and methodically as teaching academic content" (80). When rules and procedures are taught, children are more on task and exhibit less problem behavior (Gettinger and Kohler 2006; Kern and Clemens 2007). Yet, it's normal that at some point in time all children will misbehave. Effective teachers do not view misbehavior as an inherent flaw of the child or that the child is just trying to get under their skin. Effective teachers view these occurrences of misbehavior as opportunities to teach children. Children may misbehave because they lack the skill or self-regulation needed to behave appropriately (Carter and Doyle 2006; Hester, Hendrickson, and Gable 2009). Children may misbehave to avoid doing a task they do not (or perceive they do not) have the skill to complete (Bambara and Knoster 2009). Children may also go about getting what they want in an inappropriate way, which Carter and Doyle (2006) refer to as a "manifestation of misplaced goals" (394). When children misbehave, it is critical that we teach children a better way to act through redirection and that we are consistent in our follow-through.

Simply stating a rule like "Be nice, be safe" is not sufficient. We have to explain, model, *and* have children practice (Gettinger and Kohler 2006). First, we need to explain what the rules and the procedures mean and why they are important. This includes giving students clear examples of what it means to follow the rule/procedure (Carter and Doyle 2006). For example, students can brainstorm what "Be nice, be safe" looks like, sounds like, feels like during different times of the day. "Being nice" may mean sharing your pencil with your classmate but not saying that someone can't play with you at recess. "Being safe" may mean walking but not running when getting in line at the door. Then, you and students can model or role-play what it means to follow the rules (Elias and Schwab 2006). You may call on several students to model how to walk to get in line at the door and discuss the key behaviors (e.g., walking, taking shortest route from desk to door). Then, *all* students should have the opportunity to practice following the rule (Bohn, Roehrig, and Pressley 2004). During this practice time, you should reinforce the key behaviors when the student follows the rule/procedure. If a student has difficulty, you should remind the student of the expected behavior and have the student practice again.

This needs to happen on more than just the first day of school (Carter and Doyle 2006)! This process of explaining, modeling, and practicing needs to occur until students have mastered following the expectation (Leinhardt, Weidman, and Hammond 1987). Just like you wouldn't expect students to master single-digit addition in one lesson, you should not expect them to master "Be nice, be safe" in one presentation. Instruction on how to follow a rule needs to be presented several times. Teaching all rules and procedures on the first day would be information overload to students (Emmer, Evertson, and Anderson 1980), so instead start with the rules and procedures that are most "related to the child's immediate needs" (228), such as the rules critical to forming a classroom community (e.g., using kind words) or procedures, such as where to store backpacks and requesting to use the bathroom. Lewis, Sugai, and Colvin (1998) illustrate that teachers can also use creative strategies to embed teaching rules and procedures during content-area time, such as having students write stories about characters who follow (or don't follow) the classroom rules or making posters that illustrate how to follow the rules.

Reinforce Positive Behavior with Specific Praise. Another evidenced-based classroom management is praise (also known as *social reinforcement*). When students are effectively praised, their rate of positive behavior increases (Chalk and Bizo 2004; Kern and Clemens 2007). Praise provides feedback for students, which builds students' feelings of competence (Reeve 2006). That is, students who receive positive feedback have better views of their behavior and ability (Chalk and Bizo 2004; Montague and Rinaldi 2001). Also, by verbally noticing what students are doing well, you are communicating to them that they are a valued part of the classroom community, which instills a sense of belonging and relatedness.

You may say, "Yes, of course! I praise my students all the time." Yet, research may indicate otherwise. One team of researchers found that teachers reprimanded three times as often as they praised (Sutherland and Wehby 2001). In fact, some researchers found that even when children with challenging behavior exhibited compliance and on-task behavior, they were rarely reinforced for that positive behavior (Van Acker, Grant, and Henry 1996)! That's a bleak picture but the good news is that Sutherland and Wehby also found that when teachers kept a record of their use of praise, they increased their praise statements and decreased their reprimands. In other words, our limited use of praise is something that we can change in our classrooms by increasing our awareness of how we speak to children. According to Kern and Clemens (2007), teachers should provide praise four times as often as they provide corrective feedback (almost the reverse ratio of what teachers tend to do). For one hour, I encourage you to record the number of times you praise versus reprimand children in your classroom. If you are not praising four times as often as you are reprimanding or redirecting children's behavior, you now have a concrete goal to work toward.

It is also important to be aware of how you praise. There are principles to using praise effectively (Bohn, Roehrig, and Pressley 2004; Chalk and Bizo 2004; Hester, Hendrickson, and Gable 2009; Kern and Clemens 2007; Stormont, Smith, and Lewis 2007). First, praise should always be **sincerely delivered**. Second, you should provide praise **immediately** following the appropriate behavior. Third, praise should be **specific**. Rather than a global, nondescript "Good job," your praise should make clear to the student what she has done well. For instance, "Maria, I noticed that you put your book bag in your cubby without being asked this morning." Fourth, praise is more effective when you are **physically close** to the child you are praising. Making **eye contact** with the student is also reinforcing. Using these principles, you can deliver praise to individual students, several students, or the entire class (Kern and Clemens 2007).

Another consideration is that when a child is mastering a new behavior, you should praise the child every time you see him doing it (Hester, Hendrickson, and Gable 2009). When the child has a pretty good grasp on the behavior, then you can back your praise down to intermittent use, perhaps every few times the child exhibits the behavior. It is also important to realize that children are different. Not all children welcome praise . . . or welcome praise in the context that you gave it. For some children, they may feel embarrassed or may not want to be singled out for attention (Hester, Hendrickson, and Gable 2009). You may need to deliver praise privately versus publicly.

Remind Students of Expectations. Students benefit from periodic reminders about expectations (Emmer, Evertson, and Anderson 1980; Mayer 1995). Effective teachers remind students what the expectations are before the task is begun to *prevent* problem behavior (Stormont, Smith, and Lewis 2007). You may also hear this referred to as *precorrection*. When students are reminded, problem behavior decreases (Lewis, Sugai, and Colvin 1998; Stormont, Smith, and Lewis 2007). You may remind the students, such as "Remember that we need to walk slowly and quietly when we line up to go to music class." Or you may ask a student to remind the class of the expectations, such as "Stephanie, remind us how we are supposed to line up to go to music class." This technique also works well to make sure students understand the directions for independent work. If students forget the steps of the directions, then they will be off task and more likely to misbehave.

Redirect Disruptive Behavior. When students are not following the rules or procedures, teachers should redirect students using the following guidelines (Matheson and Shriver 2005; Walker and Sylwester 1998). First, **immediately** redirect them. Effective classroom managers stop misbehavior promptly before classroom activities are disrupted (Carter and Doyle 2006; Emmer, Evertson, and Anderson 1980). Redirections should be delivered in **positive and direct language**. That is, tell the student what he should be doing, such as "Michael, walk." If you say "Michael, don't run," perhaps Michael is allowed to skip or hop? Obviously, that is a silly example, but you get the idea. You take the unknown out of the request when you tell students what to do versus what not to do. Redirections also need to be **concise**. For instance, "Michael, walk" rather than "Michael, you need to walk because if you go too fast, you could trip or bump into one of your friends." Remember that you should have already taught the rules and explained why they are in place, so redirections should be short and to the point. (Note: If you do find that a rule/procedure is consistently violated, you should explicitly reteach it to an individual student or to the whole class.) Also, make sure you **give the student enough time to comply with the request**. When students do comply, remember to praise!

One habit that you may need to break is making requests in the form of a question, like "Michael, can you please sit down?" These are called *indirect commands*. Some students, particularly low-income and ethnic-minority students, have not had experience with indirect commands (Morine-Dershimer 2006). They may not comply with your request—not out of disrespect but because they legitimately think you are asking them a question and that it is a reasonable response to say "no." Therefore, when you are redirecting students, you should make a declarative **statement**, not form it as a question.

Other points to consider when redirecting students is that requests need to be delivered in a **calm and respectful**—not angry or overly loud—tone of voice (Matheson and Shriver 2005; Rhode, Jenson, and Morgan 2009). Just like when delivering praise, using **eye contact** and **being physically close** to the child are more effective (Emmer, Evertson, and Anderson 1980; Rhode, Jenson, and Morgan 2009).

Provide Appropriate Consequences. When students do not follow the rules, the research is very clear that there need to be consistent and relevant consequences (Bohn, Roehrig, and Pressley 2004; Gettinger and Kohler 2006). Thompson (2004) discusses that this may be particularly true for African American students who will lose respect for a teacher they consider to be weak. Consequences should be reasonable, tied to the misbehavior, and delivered calmly and privately (Elias and Schwab 2006; Landrum and Kauffman 2006). You should not have the same consequence, such as a phone call home, for every situation of misbehavior. Let's say Jonathon teases Javier. The teacher sentences Jonathon to losing recess for three days. This is both an unreasonable length of time and not related to the misbehavior—notwithstanding the research that tells us students need the physical activity during recess! Instead, Jonathon's consequence could be to assist Javier in carrying the kickballs out to recess—this consequence is considered an "apology of action" (Brady et al. 2003). Effective consequences should permit children to reflect on more appropriate behavior (Elias and Schwab 2006; Watson and Battistich 2006). We need to break the mind-set that consequences always have to be punishment or a way to "teach this kid a lesson." When I "teach a lesson," my goal is for students to learn, so if possible, I structure consequences so that children are practicing more positive behavior.

The majority of teachers use time-outs. When used appropriately, time-outs are effective in reducing negative behavior in students (Turner and Watson 1999). Time-outs should be used to provide the student a breather to reflect on her behavior and regain self-control. Time-outs should not be to punish the child. (Remember that like any procedure, time-outs should be explicitly taught to students using the procedures described earlier in this section.) Often, teachers use time-outs or "take a break" procedures in the classroom, where the child remains in the classroom but is removed from the activity at hand. When the child is able to view what the class is doing, this is called *nonexclusionary time-out* (Harris 1985). In this type of time-out, the child can learn from watching the appropriate behaviors being displayed by her peers. It is important for the teacher to reinforce these appropriate peer behaviors to make learning explicit for the child in time-out. Teachers may also elect to use an exclusionary time-out whereby the student remains in the classroom but is not able to see what the rest of the class is doing, such as sitting at a desk positioned where the student faces away from the classroom (Harris 1985). This may be most effective if the student's misbehavior is related to getting peer attention (Turner and Watson 1999). (If using an exclusionary time-out, make sure you can see the student so you can monitor her behavior.) Regardless of the type of time-out used, it is important that the teacher monitor the child and reinforce the child's displays of positive behaviors when the child rejoins the class (Turner and Watson 1999). Some teachers also encourage students to put themselves in time-out when students are feeling out of control. Although there are no research findings to indicate the specific effectiveness of this procedure, it is intuitively appealing because of its promotion of children's social competence in the areas of self-awareness, self-management, and responsible decision making. In the case of very disruptive behavior, having the student take a "time-out" in another teachers' classroom or office is also effective (Watson and Battistich 2006). Based on a review of empirical findings, Turner and Watson (1999) recommend time-outs initially be no longer than five minutes. If shorter time-outs are not effective for a student, longer time-out periods can be employed. Teachers should be cautious about the use of time-out, both in and out of the classroom. Some students may misbehave in order to avoid the situation (e.g., child struggles in math so does not want to do the math activity), so sending them (or allowing them to go) to time-out may inadvertently be reinforcing their misbehavior! Also, when students are not in your classroom, they are missing valuable instructional time.

On a related note, school suspensions (in-school and out-of-school) are a very common discipline strategy (Allman and State 2011; Chin et al. 2012). When suspended, students are missing a prolonged amount of class time. This is problematic because students who are suspended are typically students who are already struggling academically; as a result of the suspension, these students fall further behind, leading them to low school engagement and more negative behavior (Allman and State 2011; Chin et al. 2012; Hemphill and Hargreaves 2009). Additionally, students who are suspended are likely to be suspended in the future (Chin et al. 2012), further indicating that suspensions are not an effective mechanism to reduce challenging behaviors.

When More Is Needed

The strategies discussed here will suffice for approximately 80 to 90 percent of students (Epstein et al. 2008). However, the remaining students will need more intensive support. The process I will briefly describe here is referred to as a *function-based intervention*. For more information, see Wood and Ferro (2012), who provide in teacher-friendly language a more thorough description as well as helpful resources. Additionally, even though at first glance this process may seem complex, teachers have indicated that following this protocol was feasible for them to do and more importantly an effective procedure to increase positive behavior (Lane et al. 2006).

Figure Out the Why

The most critical question to address is why the problem behavior is occurring (Bambara and Knoster 2009; Epstein et al. 2008). Consider Celia, who hits her classmates during group work. Knowing the why will allow us to better identify the pro–social skill that Celia needs to work on and how we can best support that. If Celia is hitting because she wants the materials her classmates are using during group work time, teaching her to politely ask her classmates to share is indeed a fitting alternative behavior. However, what if Celia is hitting to get out of group work because the content is too difficult for her? In this case, we may teach her to use a signal to alert you that she needs assistance with the material.

In order to figure out the why, we need to observe Celia to identify what behavioral analysts call the **antecedents** and **consequences** of the behavior (Bambara and Knoster 2009; Epstein et al. 2008; Umbreit et al. 2007). *Antecedents* refer to the triggers that set off the behavior. For instance, it could be that the behavior most often occurs during group work or right before lunch when the student is hungry or during math or with a certain classmate, and so on. *Consequences* refer to what happens immediately after the student displays the behavior, such as the student yells, the teacher reprimands. Students typically misbehave to either **get something** (like teacher attention, even if it is negative) or to **avoid something** (like getting out of math because the content is difficult; Epstein et al. 2008; Umbreit et al. 2007). When we don't accurately put these pieces together (**A**ntecedents lead to **B**ehavior lead to **C**onsequences, or **ABC**), we may be accidentally reinforcing and increasing the problem behavior (Mayer 1995)! Classic example: Sammy frequently teases several of his classmates. After a warning, the teacher sends him to time-out. When we figure out the ABC, we determine that Sammy teases several of his classmates during math time, a difficult subject for him, and the teacher's consequence has allowed him to reach his goal of avoiding math. The more math he misses, the more he will want to avoid math because he is getting farther behind, the more he will disrupt the math lesson so he can avoid math, the more he is sent to time-out (or the principal's office) . . . you get the idea. This is a perpetuating cycle that must be broken.

Before we begin our observation, we first need to determine what behaviors to observe. Some students present numerous problematic behaviors. Bambara and Knoster (2009) recommend starting with one or two behaviors. They provide a helpful hierarchy of how to select the most critical behaviors to reduce: (1) destructive or harmful behaviors (such as hitting classmates) followed by (2) disruptive behaviors that interfere with the student's/classmates' learning (such as repeatedly calling out during lessons), and finally (3) distracting behaviors (such as getting out one's desk during independent work time). If a cluster of behaviors routinely occur together—such as the student gets out of his seat, walks around the room, and talks loudly to his classmates— then this cluster can be treated as one behavior. After determining the behavior or behaviors that are most critical, we need to define the behavior in terms of what is observable and measureable (Bambara and Knoster 2009; Epstein et al. 2008). We can't concretely observe "aggression" but we can observe "hits or yells at classmates." We need to define the problem behavior in terms of "what does the student look or sound like when exhibiting problem behavior" (Bambara and Knoster 2009, 25).

Before setting off on your mission to track the frequency and specific circumstances of the behavior in your classroom, first take a step back and think about this behavior more generally. Interviewing parents is a valuable way to gain a broader perspective of the child (Bambara and Knoster 2009; Wood and Ferro 2012). Does this child exhibit this behavior at home? If so, what are the circumstances? What have parents done that has (or has not) helped the child act more appropriately? Also, consider whether this misbehavior could be due to a differing cultural practice or something going on for the student outside of school (Bambara and Knoster 2009; Epstein et al. 2008). For instance, does the student demonstrate noncompliance when the activity is competitive? This could be related to their cultural beliefs. Based on her research, Thompson (2004) discusses that many African American students speak in loud voices and are outspoken, which is often interpreted as being defiant and questioning teachers' authority. Could the behavior be explained due to the child going through a difficult life circumstance, like parental divorce, death of a loved one, parental loss of employment? Understanding that a child's life circumstance contributes to negative behavior does not imply that you give the child free reign. Knowing the origins of the behavior gives you a more holistic view of the child, which promotes the development of a positive relationship. You should still use the strategies described in this book to support the child in exhibiting more positive behavior.

After defining the behavior(s), we now need to watch for the behavior and take notes on what is happening before the behavior occurs (antecedents) and what follows the behavior (consequences; Epstein et al. 2008). You may already have a good idea of when the behavior occurs and when to observe, such as opening circle/meeting or recess. However, sometimes it may feel like the behavior is "all the time." If that is the case, observe for samples of time across various activities and routines (Wood and Ferro 2012). For instance, every twenty or so minutes, you can observe the student's performance and briefly record what she is doing (Lane et al. 2006). Bambara and Knoster (2009) recommend observing until you can determine a typical pattern to the behavior.

When the student exhibits the behavior, record quick notes to yourself on: (1) time of day (e.g., morning, before lunch, end of day), (2) the setting (e.g., classroom reading area, cafeteria, recess), (3) subject area (e.g., math, science, reading), (4) type/structure of activity (e.g., whole group, small group, individual), (5) difficulty of the task, and (6) presence of specific individuals (e.g., teacher, assistant, specific peers). Also, record what happens after the child exhibits the behavior, paying particular attention to what the child may be getting or avoiding.

A Positive Behavior Exchange

Now that we have a better understanding of why the problem behavior occurs, it is time to "exchange" the problem behavior for a positive behavior. Consistent with the strategies discussed earlier, the emphasis should be on the positive—teaching and reinforcing prosocial alternative behaviors to replace the problem behavior (Mayer 1995). This is called the "fair-pair" rule. When there is a behavior that we want to reduce or eliminate, we pair it with alternative better behavior that we want to increase (Hojnoski, Gischlar, and Missall 2009). First, we have to **define the target or replacement behavior(s)**, the behavior we want the student to exhibit. Next, we need to ask ourselves whether the child has the skills to currently perform the replacement behavior and/or whether we need to improve the classroom environment or our instruction to elicit more positive behavior from the child (Wood and Ferro 2012).

Consider this example. It is the beginning of the year and one of your newly entering third graders is Demetrius, who has a long history of misbehavior. When you begin systematically observing his behavior, you form a hypothesis that he hits his classmates to avoid taking part in the reading lesson. You further discover that Demetrius's reading abilities are far below his peers. Thus, Demetrius' misbehavior may be due to lack of reading skill. An appropriate response is to provide Demetrius with extra reading instruction and/or design reading lessons in which Demetrius can be successful, even shine. For example, perhaps Demetrius has a lot of background knowledge about snakes. A reading lesson might employ texts about snakes (which he is likely to be able to read at a higher level than other texts) and Demetrius might be referred to as our "snake expert." Or let's return to our friend Celia. Celia's target behavior is to ask her classmates politely (using *please, thank you*) to share their materials during group work. When you reflect on your classroom environment, you may realize that you have never taught students your expectations and the procedures for sharing materials. Thus, an appropriate response is to explain, explicitly model, and practice these procedures. Having Celia role-play for the class how to share materials would provide her with a sense of needed competence.

If the child has the skill *and* you are using effective and developmentally appropriate practices, then an appropriate action is to create a plan so the student is reinforced for using the target behavior. You and the student (and we recommend the parent[s] as well) should develop the behavior plan together. The behavior plan should include various components (Akin-Little et al. 2004; Rhode, Jenson, and Reavis 1993). This plan should **explicitly state the target behavior** and **establish how frequently** the student must demonstrate the target behavior. It should also include the **reward or reinforcement** the student will receive when he has met the behavioral expectations. For instance, Celia and her teacher determine that if she exhibits her target behavior (politely asks her classmates to share their materials during group work) at least one time per group work session, she will be allowed to either pass out the materials needed for the next activity or select a new pencil from the basket.

When Rewards Make Sense

Earlier you read that rewards or reinforcers can be used to control students' behavior and undermine their intrinsic motivation. Yet, if used properly and in the right situations, rewards support students who don't yet have the internal motivation to perform this new task you are asking of them (Akin-Little et al. 2004). Demetrius may need rewards as a jump start to his motivation to break his engrained pattern of misbehavior and to be vulnerable enough to demonstrate his reading challenges.

A "golden rule" of rewards, according to teacher educators, is that they should be inexpensive, not take a lot of time, and whenever possible be natural to the environment (e.g., teacher praise, caring for a classroom pet, decorating classroom, sit by a friend, use of special classroom materials like markers and art supplies; Rhode, Jenson, and

Reavis 1993). Rewards will differ between children, which is why it is so important to include children in the development of the plan. For instance, children on the autism disorder spectrum will very likely not find special attention from a teacher to be reinforcing. Certainly, some children may prefer things like stickers and pencils (remember: inexpensive!). Whenever you provide the reinforcement, you should provide feedback to the child about what specifically he has done well (Landrum and Kauffman 2006; Reeve 2006). For instance, "Celia, I noticed that you said 'thank you' to James when he handed you the purple marker you asked for." Additionally, reinforcement is not something you should use to coerce or bribe the student. Instead, reinforcement provides feedback to the student that he successfully exhibited his target behavior (Reeve 2006). Not acceptable: "James, if you can read your assigned book quietly, remember you get an extra five minutes of recess." Acceptable: "James, I saw how you worked hard to sound out the words in your book. You earned your extra five minutes of recess today." Also, just like praise, reinforcement should be delivered immediately following the child's positive behavior (Rhode, Jenson, and Reavis 1993).

Another point to keep in mind is that how rewards or reinforcement are given should change as the child gains more competence (Akin-Little et al. 2004, Rhode, Jenson, and Reavis 1993). When the child is learning a new skill, the reinforcement should be continuous, meaning every time the child exhibits the behavior. As the child gains more skill, then the reinforcement can be "thinned" or not provided as frequently. So as Celia gets more skilled at politely asking her classmates to share, she will receive the reinforcer at the end of the week when she exhibits this behavior 80 percent of the time (versus daily).

When a Behavior Plan Isn't Working
Sometimes after beginning a behavior plan, a student's behavior will actually worsen—referred to as *rebound effect* (Epstein et al. 2008). Persevere! Epstein and colleagues (2008) recommend following the

plan for a month. Continue to record notes on the students' behavior, antecedents, and consequences. If after a month the plan is not successful, you will have more data to determine how the plan should be modified. However, if you are still really struggling with students after employing all of these strategies, this is the time to employ a team approach (Epstein et al. 2008). Discuss the situation with your administration, guidance counselor, school psychologist, or others. A more thorough assessment may need to be conducted. In addition, the school psychologist or guidance counselor may provide additional social skills sessions to support the student. For instance, maybe you have a student who needs explicit instruction on how to read body language or identify how she is feeling (Jones and Bouffard 2012). Social skills training has been very effective in reducing problem behavior and increasing positive behavior (e.g., Brown et al. 2004; Freiberg and Lapointe 2006).

A State of Responsiveness and Caring

As you've seen, classroom management is not about managing "bad" kids, but about recognizing why kids behave in certain ways and giving them the tools to be their best selves. Rather than being drawn into the negative emotional state of a child causing the bad behavior, we have to be responsive to the conditions that create it. In the next section, Gianna will give you more detail on how these tools play out in the everyday life of classrooms. Through the presentation of familiar scenarios, she will extend your thinking about how to create a classroom management system that is based in caring relationships, rather than authority and control.

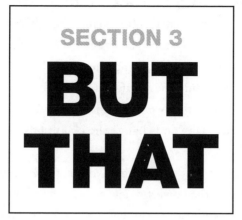

SECTION 3

BUT THAT

A Better Way

GIANNA CASSETTA

If you are falling . . . dive.
—Joseph Campbell

In Section 2, Brook explained why a rewards and consequences system doesn't work and the better practices teachers can use instead. Before thinking about how to put those in place, it's important to acknowledge that many schools in the United States function with no schoolwide classroom management practices. Others adopt ones that are one-size-fits-all. How does the solitary teacher navigate a new path? What can teachers do when they reach a pivot point and realize, "I know this isn't working but I don't know what to do instead." This section focuses on classroom management practices that any individual teacher can implement in any school. Instead of allowing ourselves to fall, let's dive in to some better practices.

Never Blame the Lettuce: Developing the Mind-Set Toward Giving Rather Than Taking Away

Buddhist monk Thich Nhat Hanh explains that, "When you plant lettuce, if it does not grow well, you don't blame the lettuce. You look into the reasons it is not doing well. It may need fertilizer, or more water, or less sun. You never blame the lettuce" (1991, 78). The same is true of children. Instead of blame, we as teachers must look for reasons why children are not behaving and change the conditions to set students up for success.

Always remember that as a teacher, you, not the child, are in a position of power. If you, the powerful one, are uncomfortable about a child's behavior, imagine the distress the child must be feeling. It is that distress that is likely causing the misbehavior. Trust that the child is doing the best with the tools she has, and that you need to figure out what tools she really needs in order to become a responsible decision maker.

You must embrace that you are both the problem and the solution. Although I know that is a hard pill to swallow, it is a pill that the most effective teachers have swallowed a long time ago. Let's view this in the most positive light. When classroom management issues occur, it simply means you need to figure out what you are doing to either cause the problem or allow the problem to persist. And then you need to change what you are doing. Only you, the teacher, have the power to resolve classroom management issues.

For the research on how classroom behavior and academic performance are linked

see Section 2, page 20

Understanding Why Students Misbehave

When students break rules, we must look for the gap in social skill development. We must teach explicitly and often in order to meet the fundamental needs that we all share: relatedness, autonomy, and competence. As Brook has shared, if these needs are met in our classroom, then children will have the necessary foundation to be successful in school and beyond.

Absence of a Sense of Belonging

Many children view school as central to their lives. It is where they spend much of their childhood. It is where their friends are, where there are adults who care about them, where they learn, play, and generate. They have positive relationships with others, they have a sense of personal efficacy, and they have fun at school. For those children, when they arrive at school, they feel like they belong there and are valued members of their school and classroom community. Because they belong, those children have an enhanced sense of confidence and self-worth, and as a result, they generally "behave" at school and learn more. As many of us have experienced, when children "behave," teachers' perceptions of student academic abilities are more positive, whether those perceptions are true or not.

But not all children are fortunate enough to have this experience. For some children, the classroom setting exacerbates their feelings of alienation, rejection, and failure. As Brook discussed in Section 2, when children do not have strong relationships with their teachers and classmates, it significantly decreases their sense of belonging. Children from low-income and ethnic-minority backgrounds and boys are less likely to have positive relationships with teachers at school. These children are more likely to misbehave in school.

> **For the research on which students are most often in need of positive teacher–student relationships**
>
> see Section 2, page 25

It is important to call out that teachers, the adults and the professionals, have the power to build relationships with children and to help them see school as a place that is for them. It is critical to make every effort to build relationships and to be purposeful about helping all children see school as a place where they belong.

Teacher Perceptions Based on Race, Class, and Gender. One of the schoolwide responses to misbehavior at my school is a procedure we call "office take a break," which we refer to as *OTAB*. As teachers are developing their own skills at teaching social competencies, OTAB is a support for teachers who may have power struggles with students. OTAB is a fifteen-minute break, where a student comes to a designated spot in the office to de-escalate and regain control.

We track all OTAB data to analyze on a monthly basis. Like most schools in America, our data showed that African American boys were "disciplined" through the use of OTAB at a shockingly higher rate than any other group of students. For a school that prides itself on the balance between teaching social and academic skills, this simply was not an acceptable finding. But it was important to understand why it occurred in order to change things.

Our school, like many others, is one staffed by a disproportionate number of young, middle-class, white women. The reality is, we have different cultural norms than many of the children we teach, and not having ever been a boy, we often simply don't "get" boys, especially African American boys.

It is critical that we acknowledge the reality of the preconceptions we bring into the classroom—we all have them. If we are honest with ourselves, and intentionally monitor our thoughts and our actions, we can recognize when we are not treating particular groups of students "fairly." In my own school, through a process of honest conversations and self-study, we have slowly begun shifting our own negative data to show more democratic and fair use of procedures.

Academic Frustrations

For the research linking academic performance to student behavior

see Section 2, page 20

Although it is sometimes difficult to recognize, our own skill at delivering engaging and differentiated academic instruction is often the cause of misbehavior. Students who are frustrated with the work—it is too boring, too difficult, or they simply don't understand—will often act out as a way of avoiding the work.

Parker, a sassy fourth grader, entered my class as the student who "ran the school." He was still struggling through books with a simple, repetitive line on each page with heavy picture support. The reading instruction he had received up to this point was frustrating for him. It didn't keep him engaged, so he found lots of other ways to entertain himself. Parker needed a few things to happen.

High Academic Expectations with Differentiated, Scaffolded Instruction. Parker needed to be engaged in much higher-level work—it wasn't enough for teachers to give him what he considered "baby books" and suggest only a single strategy to use in tackling these books. For example, he needed to be interacting with sophisticated texts and concepts—but needed to hear them first read aloud, sometimes several times, and sometimes again with the support of a partner reader.

Engagement and Differentiation Through Choice. It was critical for Parker to have some choice about his learning. During independent reading and centers, and as an independent writing project, Parker wanted to learn more about endangered animals. He needed to be able to collect content information from texts, photographs, talking to others and through field trips and video clips. This choice, as well as the variety of resources from which he could gather information, gave him the buy-in he needed to grow his content knowledge and apply it to his reading and writing.

Planned Activities with Children's Attention Span in Mind. At the start of my work with Parker, his interactions with any given reading task had to be short—while others might be able to go for thirty to forty minutes of sustained independent work, Parker would need to have two separate work sessions planned with a break in between. With this approach, he was able to build stamina over time.

Every classroom has one if not five Parkers. As teachers, we must accept that we can't expect the child to shift needs in order to meet our expectations—it would be setting ourselves up for an unwinnable battle. Rather, we must focus on shifting instruction to meet the student's needs.

If you have a student who is experiencing academic frustration

- Let the child know you see the struggles and will support him.
- Use age- and interest-appropriate materials, not just level-appropriate materials.
- Make sure the child has some input or choice about topics of study.
- Pay attention to how long the child can work before needing a break and adjust as necessary.

What we often don't realize is that many of our students have learned to "play school," or fake it. They are compliant, they appear to be listening, they go through the routines and procedures of the work. As my own son recently said, "I have no idea what our read-aloud book is about. But I sit there, for like, thirty minutes so I don't get in trouble." Consistently self-check that you are teaching to student needs, not teaching them to play to yours.

Developmental Differences

Because knowledge of child development is such a critical factor in how we perceive student behavior, in this final section on understanding the why, we are going to look at three typical classroom problems. In the wrong hands, the children involved would be viewed as misbehaving. As such, we will look at some typical teacher responses that are not grounded in child development. We will also look at plan development in the hands of a teacher who understands childhood development, who believes what the students are doing is pretty normal for their age and are highly teachable.

The Noisy First Graders. First graders are typically in the six- to seven-year-old range. First graders may be described as enthusiastic, eager, imaginative, and even boisterous. Six-year-olds in particular are experiencing a dramatic shift in cognitive growth and tend to be highly social, and as a result, they are experimenting with language in new and exciting ways. Exciting, at least to the first graders. And here lies the problem. To the classroom teacher, the problem is how to get the first graders to stop talking.

Bob's first-grade class had lots of energy. To Bob, it often felt like too much energy. He described his students as "wiggly" and often joked with them about having ants in their pants. Although he had fantastic relationships with his students and knew them well as individuals, he was growing increasingly frustrated by the incessant chatter and constant interruptions while he was teaching. He had taught first grade before and knew them to be talkative. Maybe because this class was a little bigger, or maybe because of the combination of personalities, this group was especially challenging for Bob.

Some Typical Responses

- Clamp down. Get very strict and authoritative about talking and moving. Practice and practice again behavioral expectations until the children are still and quiet.
- Seat some students who are more disruptive at the carpet at individual seats.

While this may be effective short term, it won't last. Developmental needs in first graders aren't and shouldn't be easily squelched.

Setting the goals with students. After discussing the issue with colleagues and administrators, and naming the issue for his class, they set two goals together:

1. Continue to have fun learning.
2. Be clear with each other about when it is okay to talk and when it is not okay to talk.

Setting a plan in action. Bob proceeded with a plan knowing that he must give in to the need for first graders to talk and to socialize, but he wanted to make sure it did not persist through every moment of the day. So he decided to create more opportunities for talk, but also to be clear and firm about quiet times. And he limited the quiet times to direct instruction—in other words, no talking while he was talking. So he tried the following plan.

If you have noisy first graders

- Break thirty minutes of recess into two, fifteen-minute recess periods—one midmorning and one midafternoon.

- Add frequent turn and talks into lessons, and be very firm and direct about students turning off the talk in between.

- Build a turn and talk into independent reading and writing, so students could talk to each other about their work.

- Make most math work group work.

- Build a song and movement activity in between each lesson.

- Add a five-minute social time to afternoon snack.

Within two weeks, Bob felt successful. When I asked him why, he reflected that students were probably spending more minutes overall talking than they were before, but now he was able to get them quiet and focused when he needed it. In other words, now he was being responsive to the students instead of not trying to control it.

The Competitive Third Graders. When students reach third grade they are typically in the eight- to nine-year-old range. Generally, third graders can be described as enthusiastic, energetic, and eager for the approval of peers and adults. But as third graders get older, they have a tendency to become competitive (and negative and complaining). Let's take a look at how competition manifests itself as a classroom problem.

David, Rob, and James are old friends. They've been together for a year in grade 2, and have looped up with their teacher to third grade.

They are on the older end of the grade 3 spectrum, all having turned, or about to turn, nine. In enters Kevin. He is new to the school and also nine. He is drawn to the group—they are highly physical, love sports, and enjoy playing hard together. On the playground, they pretend to be their favorite NBA players—twisting, turning, doing layups, dreaming some day they will be tall enough to dunk. In the lunchroom, they compare stats about their favorite teams. This could be the start of a strong friendship.

But pretty quickly, arguments erupt. Whose layups are more skillful? Who runs the fastest? Whose team has won the most championships? At lunch, David, a New York Knicks fan, says to Kevin, a diehard Boston Celtics fan who comes to school fully garbed in Celtics gear, "I took a poop and do you know what was in it? The Celtics." Rob and James, of course, just can't contain their laughter.

Now, to adults, this might seem trivial, amusing, or even down right hysterical. But according to child development expert and writer Chip Wood, for a nine-year-old, "Competition can be deadly serious." This was a pivot point in an all-out love–hate relationship, an emotional and physical competition between the boys. This was the start of more heated arguments, name-calling, and even some physical aggression. What is a teacher to do in such a situation?

Some Typical Responses
- Separate them. They don't interact appropriately and therefore shouldn't be together.
- Ban basketball play or talk. Competition over basketball is clearly the root of the problem.

While these responses may get the boys to "behave" and "play school" correctly, the boys will not learn a whole lot about problem solving or social skills if the teaching isn't immediate and explicit. Remember, we are always trying to help children develop the five competencies of social and emotional learning: self-awareness, self-management (impulse control), social awareness (understanding of others), relationship skills, and decision-making (problem-solving) skills.

After discussing the problem with colleagues and meeting with the boys, here was the teacher's action plan to address the situation and support the development of her students through socially responsive teaching.

If you have competitive third graders

Set Goals

1. Intentionally complement each other's skill and interests.

2. Name when something has been said that bothers them and say how it makes them feel.

Set a Plan in Action

- During choice time, which is a less structured time of day that allows children to work together at something fun and self-selected, teachers work with children on specific social skills. The teacher decided to keep whole-class choice lessons focused on the two goals, and once a week, worked specifically with this group of boys in the speed stacking center, where competition has played out at its worst.

- Once a week, during class meetings, model positive interactions that students could have during a competitive game, and then have students role-play in partnerships positive interactions they might have.

- Once a week during lunch, eat with the competitive group and engage the boys in conversation about the topic competition centers around. For example, a teacher in my school modeled naming when the conversation was getting too heated and let the boys know it made her feel uncomfortable. The boys also tried naming when similar things happened for them.

- During morning meeting and other safe, community-building times of day, play competitive games and explicitly teach how to respond when you win or lose and have fun with others.

- Give the competitive group opportunities to interact and monitor their interaction twice a week, reminding and reteaching social skills as necessary.

Like with any good teaching, teaching the boys how to have positive interactions was a process, but by the end, they had their own set of tools for building their friendship while maintaining their passion for basketball.

The Rude, Argumentative Fifth Graders. Fifth graders are typically in the ten- to eleven-year-old range. They are characterized by changing bodies, hormones, and emotions. Fifth graders need to talk through their ideas, they enjoy friendships, and they can work for longer periods of time. They have an interest in issues of justice and want to explore right and wrong. For older fifth graders, they may push on the limits of authority in order to understand it, and as a result, can often be perceived by adults as argumentative or rude.

My own fifth-grade class had been together for a while. We started together when they were fourth graders. There were many strong friendships in the class and the students knew each other very well. Our class felt like a family. And as in many families, the siblings began to argue. I saw a significant shift in behavior soon after the start of grade 5, characterized by incessant bickering. "I don't like your tone!" or "That's so wrong!" or "You are getting on my last nerve." I knew enough about fifth graders to know that I had to give them a vehicle for productive argument.

Some Typical Responses

- Provide students with individual work space at all time. It will significantly reduce the possibility of arguments erupting, and it will prepare them for life in middle school.
- Reinforce that children may only speak when called on.
- Use a point system where students are penalized for talking out of turn.

None of these responses will teach the social skills that students need in order to be successful. Furthermore, these responses are inconsiderate of developmental needs.

If you have argumentative fifth graders

Set Goals

After naming the behavior I was seeing, I established the following goals with my class.

1. Learn talk moves that help us talk to each other directly but respectfully.

2. Not to argue just for the sake of it, but for a purpose and backed up by evidence.

Set a Plan in Action

I decided to use read-aloud as the launch point for teaching students how to talk and to argue. In our classroom we used the jargon "talk moves," some of which are also part of what some refer to as "accountable talk." Following are several different lists of ways we learned about "talk moves."

When we talk to each other, we are accountable to our learning community. We show it in the way that we:

- Look at each other when we talk.
- Wait for a pause in someone else's speaking before we talk.
- Speak in a clear voice.
- Lean in and turn our heads to listen.
- Ask questions so that we can clear up confusion and understand each other better.
- Let others know when we can't hear, don't understand, or need clarification.
- Can restate what others have said before us.

When we are accountable, we push ourselves to say more in a conversation.

When We Agree

- I understand and would like to add . . .
- That makes sense because . . .

- That's really smart because . . .

- That's true because . . .

- I like when you said that . . . because . . .

When We Disagree

- I don't think that's true because . . .

- I understand what you're saying but I have a different point of view . . .

- I know that's your opinion, but . . .

- Can you give me evidence to support your opinion?

- I don't agree with your saying that . . . because . . .

When we are accountable to our learning community, we care about what others have to contribute to the conversation.

- _____, it looks like you'd like to say something.

- Can you say more about that?

- _____, what do you think about what I said?

- Can you say that in a different way?

- So what you're saying is . . .

- Can we all try to find evidence of this in the text?

- Why do you think that?

By midyear, there were clear signs of success. The class had been listening to Angela Johnson's *Humming Whispers* (1995), a book about a thirteen-year-old girl, Sophie, who is afraid of "catching" schizophrenia from her older sister, Nicole. At the point we are at in the novel, Sophie, who is responsible for looking after Nicole while her aunt is at work, has begun to steal things. She has begun to seem sulky and withdrawn. When the class noticed these changes in Sophie's behavior, they began to wonder why.

Two of the things we were working on in our discussions was being able to talk with a controlling idea (no more random bickering) and holding people accountable to saying things that make sense and that are on topic (sophisticated arguments from the eleven-year-olds!). I knew we were okay because we had learned to have discussions like this:

"So guys, we've started noticing lots of changes in Sophie lately—she's stealing, she's moody, she sulks a lot. Not the same, happy responsible kid we knew at the beginning of the book. And I've heard some of you talking about what might be bringing about these changes in her."

For research on the five competencies of social and emotional learning that can be fostered by this kind of student-led discussion

see Section 2, page 19

Before we began talking about the book, I reminded students, "When we begin our conversation, I need you to do two things: First, I need you only to talk about your theory about Sophie and how and why you think what you think. We're talking about one thing today, and that's what it is. Are we clear on that? Okay. Second, if you hear someone saying something that doesn't quite make sense, I need you to hold them accountable to making sense. You can use the chart up there about different ways we can hold each other accountable to making sense. Somebody say back to me what we're doing today . . . great. Anyone can start the conversation, so whenever you are ready. . . ."

Juan-Diego: I think Sophie is stealing because she's jealous of Nicole. I think Sophie is stealing because she's jealous of all the attention Nicole is getting, so I think she's stealing to get some attention for herself.

August: Has anyone here ever considered the possibility that she might actually be getting schizo-whatever-you-macallit? I think she is acting a little crazy.

Latrell: August, can you find a place in the text where you see that, 'cause I don't agree with you. (August picks up a book and begins to flip through and after a few moments gives up.) She's, she's just a little messed up. Her parents are dead, she's got a lot of responsibilities for someone her age. I'm not saying what she's doing is right, she's just, you know, what's the word?

Mike: Stressed.

Latrell: Yeah, she's stressed.

Mike: What I've been thinking is, you know how Sophie is scared that she's gonna get what her sister has? So I think Sophie might be testing herself. To see if she's really got the disease.

Latrell: Interesting.

Jem: Mike, could you say more about that?

Mike: Like, she's putting herself in these situations, like stealing things, to see how she'll react. Like to see how much control she has of herself. I don't know if that makes sense yet. I just started thinking it.

Jem: Now that's deep.

The Toolbox

If you only have a hammer, you tend to see every problem as a nail.
—Abraham Maslow

I've worked with so many teachers over the years who in times of frustration have said, "I've used everything in my toolbox, nothing is working!" But really, they've lost sight of their toolbox. The real classroom management toolbox isn't full of bold, flashy moves, but with tools defined by care, simplicity, and consistency. You have already learned reasons why students misbehave—a critical tool for any classroom teacher. In this section are other critical tools for managing a classroom effectively. Know that each time you use a classroom management tool with consistency, you are also giving your students tools for developing the five competencies of social and emotional learning: self-awareness, self-management, social awareness, relationship skills, and decision-making skills.

Make Rules That Mean Something

In Section 2, Brook gave us guidelines for rule creation. In this section, I repeat those guidelines, explaining how they play out in my school.

Rules Should Be Positive. In our school, we focus on broadly stated rules, to which every imaginable behavior could be connected. For example, if the rule is "Take care of each other," we explore every possible way we take care of each other—use hands for sharing or kind touches, greet each other warmly, make eye contact when the other person is speaking, and the list goes on and on.

Rules Should Be Few in Number. We generally end up with three to four rules. These are usually along the lines of:
- Take care of yourself.
- Take care of each other.
- Take care of our classroom.
- Take risks.

Rules Should Be Posted. Rules are posted in every classroom and referred to often. For example, "I see several containers of paint left open. Let's remember our rule of taking care of our classroom. Head back to the paint area to close the containers tightly."

Who Should Create Rules? As Brook explained in Section 2, researchers have not reached consensus on who should create rules, but we know as adults that if we aren't invested in something, we do it halfheartedly. If we want children to truly feel competent and autonomous, they simply must have a say in the rules that guide their classroom community. When I walk into a classroom and see a rule like "Follow directions the first time it is given," I'm 99.9 percent sure that one was written without student input. How often, do you, the adult, need to be given a direction a second, or a seventh, time?

Have a Vision and Procedure for Everything

If you have a vision for what each part of the day should look like (which you must!), you can create a procedure to make your vision a reality (see Figure 3–1). For example, imagine how a perfect pack-up at the end of the day would go. Where would students be when it is time to pack up? What might they be finishing? How do they get to their bags and coats? When and how do they get the materials that go into their backpack? Do they go one at a time or in groups? How will you send them so that the flow of movement is safe and controlled? What do they do when they are finished packing up? This is your vision.

> **Why do procedures matter? For the research on how they can help**
>
> see Section 2, page 32

Artwork by Jenna Nelson

Your procedure is the order you arrange the steps in. You should be able to explain your steps in perfect order as if it is a "how-to"— in other words, first you do this, then you do this, next you do this.

Quite often, you have to try out and revise the procedure before it works perfectly. For example, teachers in my school have revised entry and pack up procedures a number of times before settling on a procedure that worked best.

Speak with Authority

There are many factors of effective communication, including tone, pacing, volume, emotion, proximity, gestures, eye contact, and syntax. You must pay attention to those factors at all times of the day, and certainly when you are giving directions or redirecting student behavior. I've seen too many teachers not "heard" by students because their delivery is just too wishy-washy. As I always say to teachers, you are the boss in your classroom, so talk like you believe it. If you don't believe it, you need to fake the belief until it becomes real!

Speaking with authority doesn't mean being mean or yelling— it does mean you are concise, precise, and firm in telling students what to do. You are giving direct and respectful commands. This might sound like:

- "You are expected to get your notebooks out right now and start writing. I'll watch as you get started."
- "Sit down crisscross on your carpet square, fold your hands in your lap, and turn your voices off immediately."
- "I'm turning the timer on. You have thirty seconds to get in your seats, make sure your chairs are carefully tucked under your tables, and begin independent reading. This transition needs to happen quietly. You may begin entering the classroom."
- "Keep your hands at your sides as you move across the room. Walk so that everyone has their own space."

Reinforce Positive Behavior

My husband has often told me that if I try to overemphasize my recognition of positive behaviors in my own children, I might strike a balance between reinforcing and redirecting them. This is true. I have to give so much more attention to giving positive feedback in order to make it measure up to the amount of correcting I do.

I see this so often in the classroom too. As Brook mentioned, teachers typically redirect student behavior significantly more than they reinforce it. That isn't because there is no positive behavior to reinforce, it is because we don't know how important it is to look for it and name it.

Reinforcing positive behavior might sound like this:

- "You are showing me that you know how to make good decisions about where to sit so that you can get your work done."
- "You chose a book that you can read fluently and understand! How does it make you feel?"
- "You were able to manage all of your materials and keep them organized through this entire writing unit. What strategies did you use to make that happen?"
- "You were able to invite others to play with you on the playground, and now every day, friends are inviting you to play!"

"With-it-ness"

"Have eyes in the back of your head." How many times have you heard veteran teachers tell you that? Silly, right? Not really.

Researcher Jacob Kounin (1970) created the term "with-it-ness." He found that teachers who most effectively managed their classrooms monitor, scan, and assess what is happening in their classrooms constantly, no matter what else they were doing at the time. These were the teachers who addressed even the slightest hint of student "misbehavior." It is almost as if they had eyes in the backs of their heads.

A colleague of mine drew the comparison to this and her work as a beach lifeguard. If she was engaged in a conversation, giving directions to a group of swimmers, or putting on a new coat of suntan lotion, her eyes were constantly scanning the water. The risks were too high.

Follow Through

Remember the old adage, "Mean what you say and say what you mean." I couldn't possibly emphasize enough how important this is in the classroom. If you tell students to do something, you must make sure they have done it. If you don't, it is the same as telling children you don't mean business.

Follow-through might sound like:

- "Rewind. Sit back at your tables and we are going to line up again the way we agreed to."
- "I'm glad you have so many friends you want to work with. But this activity will work best in pairs. Please split up into pairs. I'll be with you when you do that."
- "I see you are having trouble using the examples of kind language we just discussed, so I am going to sit next to you and help you."

Build Relationships

For the research on why relationships matter to academic performance and student behavior

see Section 2, page 22

In Section 2, Brook walked you through the research on the importance of establishing relationships with your students. To reiterate, the research was very clear. It is critical to establish positive, supportive relationships with children so that they develop socially and emotionally and so that you can effectively manage your classroom. Through trusting relationships with adults, children learn that others can be responsive to their needs—and in turn how to be responsive to the needs of others. They learn to communicate, to face challenges, and to experience and regulate emotions. And because they can do this in a classroom where they have positive relationships, it feels achievable and safe.

In the Merriam-Webster dictionary, words used to define *relationship* include *kinship, attachment, connecting, binding*. These words are intense. Relationships with children do not always happen automatically. However, there are some very manageable, straightforward ways of building relationships with students. Remember, Brook shared that relationships are less likely to be formed with boys, especially boys of color and boys who live in poverty. Be very purposeful about establishing positive relationships with the boys in your class.

Get to Know Them as People Who Have Lives Outside of the School Building, with a Diversity of Interests, Experiences, and Personalities

Invite your students to have conversations with you. Talk to students about who you are and what you like but also ask them questions about themselves and listen to their answers. Build a bank of knowledge about all students—who makes up their families, do they have pets, what are their interests outside of school, what movies do they watch, what music do they listen to? Have lunch with your students. Play with them on the playground. Sit with them on the bus ride to a field trip. Invite them in early for a cup of tea with you. When you greet children in the morning, follow up on what you have learned about them: "Is your little brother feeling better today?" or "How did the basketball game go last night?"

If establishing relationships with students isn't something that is intuitive for you, systematize it. Create a schedule for yourself of who to eat lunch with, who to play with on the playground. Make a class list of new information you have learned about students and put a check mark next to it once you have checked in with students on the playground. You have a lot of information to keep track of as a teacher, so it is appropriate to organize your work around establishing relationships in the same way that you might organize your planning in writing or math.

Make sure students know that knowing who they are matters to you, and find something, or many things, to like about every student. When you know and like your students, your heart and mind are open to supporting them and problem solving even when they misbehave. When you don't know or, even worse, don't like a student, your heart and mind are closed to them and you become focused on consequences.

Talk with and about families. Some teachers do home visits, and others, surveys; others conduct conferences in the classroom, and others, phone calls. Do what works for you, but talk to families early on about your students. Families often love to share anecdotes or information about what their children are like outside of school. Keep conversations upbeat, and keep getting to know you and your child conversations separate from any talks about problems with students.

Jennifer went through what seemed like a dramatic behavior shift toward the end of sixth grade. Her father had always been in and out of the picture but her mother, a steady and dependable presence, was getting remarried and was deep in wedding planning. Because I had built a strong relationship with her, and we talked regularly about home, I knew this impending wedding was causing lots of anxiety for Jennifer. She didn't like her new stepfather-to-be. She feared losing her mother, and the possibility of her mother and father reuniting was ending.

Had I not known Jennifer and her family, I might have perceived her as a distant, critical, unkind child. But knowing her allowed me to understand the root of her behavior and to support her; to give her some space when she needed it; to allow her to talk about her feelings when she needed to; to coach her on her interactions with peers so she didn't take her frustrations out on them; to talk to her peers about how to support Jennifer; to coach her to use her writing as a tool to both express her anger and disappointment in the men in her life but also to make room for and celebrate her mother's happiness.

If you have a student struggling with personal issues

- Let them know you notice and care.
- Give them alternative scripts when you see they are lashing out at others.
- Create outlets for them to productively express their feelings—lunch with you and close peers, writing projects, role-play.
- If your relationship with the family allows, talk with them about how you can work together to support the student.

Support Students Through "Triggers"

When we are in a "relationship," we can anticipate triggers, or antecedents to problematic behaviors. We all have students who act out in ways we can anticipate. For example, Xavier, in my fifth-grade class, had a very hard time organizing materials. He was just one of those kids who would become discombobulated when there were lots of supplies in front of him. The worst for him was writing workshop. Pens would roll off of the table; in leaning over to pick them up, he'd knock his papers to the floor; and inevitably, one or two sheets would float away under a couch, or under a bookshelf, not to be found again until the custodians cleaned over spring break.

When something like that happened, Xavier was devastated. In his mind, all his hard work was gone forever, and it was too much to recover from in a class period. His trigger was very clear to me. So anytime we got to drafting, I knew I had to support Xavier. The support was as simple as, on the first day, "Xavier, we're drafting today.

Before you do anything else, get a stapler, and staple together all the blank sheets of loose-leaf paper you think you will need to write your draft on. Write your name across the top of every sheet in case a sheet comes loose. And make sure your drafting folder is on the desk near you to tuck your draft into at the end of class, and the one pen you are going to keep in your folder will be the only pen you will use. Got it?" After the first day, a checklist and icons were introduced, taped to the front of his writing folder.

For Xavier, I reminded him of his checklist every time he drafted. Although it wasn't quick, in time, he'd look at me and say, "I know, I know. I'll make sure I use the checklist." And I'd follow with, "You did it! You kept your materials organized and now you have a complete draft to work with!" These exchanges told him that I knew him, that I cared, and that there were strategies to work through hard times—that I was his ally.

If you have a student struggling with organization

- Let the student know you have noticed and are there to help.
- Co-create procedures for organization that are simple and reduce material use.
- Remind the student to use the procedure at consistent times.
- Create a written checklist of the procedures with icons.
- Praise use of the procedure.

Keep Teaching Relevant

Why does instruction matter to how students behave?

see Section 2, page 29

A young teacher I worked with used to complain about the interpretation of relevant teaching. "Oh, yeah," she'd say. "I remember when I was a kid and the school's way of recognizing who the student were was to hold a 'multicultural week' where we had to bring in foods and artifacts from our culture. I was a black girl adopted by Jewish parents. I didn't know if my birth parents were from the United States, from Haiti, or from Africa, and I wasn't bringing in matzoh ball soup for multicultural week!"

Relevant teaching isn't about matzoh ball soup. It is about teaching in a way that allows children to share who they are as people.

Create Academic Engagement Through Choice. For example, give students opportunities to choose writing topics that are meaningful to them. You probably wouldn't want to give a writing assignment like, "Write about your summer vacation" or "Tell about a time when you baked with your grandmother" because those experiences might not hold importance for students. For learning to be relevant, there has to be a connection to the students' experience. So, instead, you might brainstorm with students topics they are interested in writing about and give them choices. Now students have choice about relevance, and as a result, you learn something about who they are.

Choose Books That Reflect Student Backgrounds and Experiences. Another example of relevant teaching is through the books we choose for the classroom. As a teacher, I made sure to choose books that reflected their interests or issues we were dealing with in the classroom. Interest might be learning more about wolves or mummification, and topics we were exploring might have been anything from building friendships or accepting differences. This allowed us to get to deep conversations about books very quickly, and students could draw on their own experience or knowledge. Talking about books is one of the most meaningful ways to get to know each other!

Start New Studies or Investigations with Student Knowledge or Perceptions. In a "farm to table" study happening at my school, teachers are launching the study with a survey. The first study has to do with student eating habits. How many times a week do they eat fast food? Who does not eat anything that comes from an animal? Who fasts for religious reasons? Whose follows a diet that is gluten-free?

By starting the study with information about the students, teachers are creating yet another opportunity to get to know them. And, they are making a strong connection for students to a study that might have otherwise seemed removed from student interests or experiences.

Tell and, More Importantly, Show Children That You Will Keep Them Safe

Children watch us and they notice if we care about how they are treated. They know if we mean what we say, and whether or not we follow through. Start the school year by letting students know that you expect everyone in your class to be treated with kindness.

For example, I have seen many teachers, particularly in upper grades, overhear but ignore hurtful remarks children make to each other. Remarks like "Four eyes" or "Stupid" or "Your lunch looks gross" or even "Shut up" simply can't go ignored. Responses as simple as "We use kind words in our classroom" is a good start. And then it is critical to give replacement language or actions. For example, you can say, "I see you are having a hard time concentrating right now, so I'd like you to tell Gavin, 'Gavin, your talking is making it hard for me to concentrate. I really need to focus on my work right now.'" In my experience, telling students you notice an unwanted behavior and giving them a positive replacement prevents most unwanted behaviors from occurring again, as long as you are specific and consistent.

As well, I've seen lack of attention paid to inappropriate touching. A small kick here, playing with someone's hair there, tapping on someone's back. For some children these experiences are annoying or uncomfortable, and they may not yet have the tools to stop it. For example, in my school, students spend many chunks of the day sitting on a carpet. Until students automatically self-check, I would start lessons with a body check. I might say something like, "Let's do a quick body check. Make sure your hands and feet are close to your own bodies. Now check that you have a small circle of space around you and aren't touching any part of anyone else. This will help you and your friends learn better." As necessary, I might talk to students individually and say something like, "Krystal, I'm going to give you your own signal for body checks. When you see me cross my arms in an *X* across my body, and I am looking at you, stop and check your body again. That signal means I see your body too close to someone else's and that you may be making them uncomfortable."

This type of feedback to students lets them know you are looking out for their emotional and physical well-being.

A Word About Suspensions and Zero Tolerance Policies

For the research on why this practice doesn't work,

see Section 2, page 41

Having done this work for so long, I know that even the most effective teachers will inevitably ask an administrator, "Why don't we just suspend this child?"

We know from research (explained in Section 2) and experience that suspensions are not an effective way to change student behavior. So in my work as a school leader, suspensions have been rare. The primary reason I suspend a student is to allow time to create a plan. Sometimes, when student behavior is consistently disruptive, short suspensions can be used to give the teacher and class a day or two to reset, while the school makes a plan for supporting and teaching the child upon her return. If a plan isn't made while the child is out, the suspension is useless.

What might that plan be? A second grader was suspended for repeatedly using racial slurs. As you might imagine, the school community and parents were very upset. Keeping the child at home for two days alone wasn't going to change anything. However, the two days were used to give staff time to craft communication to parents and to plan a series of lessons about inclusive language and behavior across the second grades that they would teach in the classroom and at the start of recess. As well, a careful monitoring plan was put in place for the three weeks after the child's return so that staff had eyes and ears open in case another incident occurred. None did.

Most often, suspensions are illogical and developmentally inappropriate. Every child and situation are different, and deserve to be treated as such. There really is no place for zero tolerance policies in schools and classrooms that understand child development and are responsive to student needs.

An Alternative Scene from a Well-Managed Classroom: Putting What You've Learned into Action

Remember the classroom scenarios from the beginning of this book? Now we will read a brief description and analysis of a very different classroom, one with socioemotional learning initiatives.

The scene: It is the beginning of choice time. Students signed up for a variety of experiences earlier in the day. There is a research center, where children are studying the mummification process. There is a how-to center, where students make kites, bookmarks, or placemats. There is a Lego center, where students can build anything they imagine, a play performance center, and a speed stacking cup center. Before the students get to work, the teacher talks to them. "Class, I know you know that lately in centers, there has been some teasing and hurtful language. For example, in the cup speed stacking center, I've heard the word *loser* being used." Several students gesture agreement. "And in the Lego center, I've heard things like, 'That's a dumb building' or 'Mine is way better than yours.' I see a lot of you nodding in agreement. Now, I've talked with some of you about it, but being careful about our language with each other is so important that I thought I should talk to all of you about it. When I talked to some of you about why this happens, there were two reasons I heard. One, because you are excited that you won a game. Two, because you want to show off the work you have done.

"I know choice time is really, really exciting, and sometimes you want to just show off how well you are doing. That is totally normal! But sometimes, the language we use can make others feel bad, and we need to make sure our language makes each other feel good and that we are taking care of each other. Now I need you to help me brainstorm some positive language we can use when we get excited that we won a game, or because we want to show off the work we've done."

After the class has brainstormed and agreed on alternate language they will use during choice time, the teacher gives explicit directions about movement to centers and materials management. She sends students off one group at a time, giving lots of positive feedback to the class on how quickly they are getting started. She settles in with the speed stacking group and begins by reviewing the language they agreed to use while playing.

Giving, Not Taking Away

Let's start with the problem: Students were using hurtful language with each other during choice time, which is a less structured period of time for children. There are a number of ways to address this problem. Some are:

1. Replace choice with a more structured experience. Take away choice altogether. The students aren't handling it well anyway.
2. Give the class a consequence—until they start using kind language across the day, there will be no choice time.
3. Give a few students a consequence. Each time they use hurtful language, they sit out of choice.

In this scenario, the teacher chose none of these options. The options above are based on the mind-set of taking away, and this teacher's mind-set is on giving. This teacher is giving the gift of social skills.

Remember how aptly Brook described the five skills for social and emotional learning and the research behind why they are important: self-awareness, self-management (impulse control), social awareness (understanding of others), relationship skills, and decision-making (problem-solving) skills. The teacher in this scenario knows children aren't born with these skills, and that she needs to very directly and consistently teach them. She also has the same tools and knowledge you were given in this book.

Reread the scenario. How is the teacher teaching each of these skills? What tools is she using? Do you have additional ideas about how she might incorporate skill instruction into her teaching?

Students Need Opportunities to Practice Behaviors

When we teach students to read, we see it as a process that takes many years, from recognizing letters and sounds, all the way to having thoughtful discussions about books. Never would we expect a child to learn how to read without many, many interactions with books and instruction. We also wouldn't expect students to learn exactly the same way and at the same pace.

Classroom management and teaching children social and emotional competencies is no different. It is a process that takes time and carefully planned, differentiated instruction. You have to be in this for the long haul in order to transform the classroom management experience for yourself and for your students.

Always remember that teaching is no ordinary adventure—you have young lives forming in your hands. Teaching is an adventure that requires a hearty "yes!" Now let's get started.

AFTERWORD

NELL K. DUKE

I am so grateful to Gianna Cassetta and Brook Sawyer for this book, not only for professional reasons, but also for personal reasons. My son has ADHD. Research (as well as my personal experience) indicates that the symptoms of ADHD can be reduced by physical exercise (e.g., Pontifex et al. 2012)—exercise one can get during recess. For children like my son, taking away recess is entirely counterproductive, rendering worse, rather than better, the very behaviors it is meant to punish or deter.

Gianna and Brook share many strategies that can keep us from ever resorting to taking away recess: a strong sense of a classroom community; trusting and caring relationships between teacher and students; careful attention to why students behave as they do; voluminous specific praise and feedback; collectively owned, concise expectations for behavior; lots of explicit instruction in how to meet those expectations; natural consequences on the now much rarer occasions when those expectations are not met; and so on.

Gianna and Brook acknowledge that for some students, even all of these measures will not be enough, and they share some of the interventions that have been shown to help students with more significant behavioral issues, such as social skills training and the fair-pair rule. One leaves with a sense of optimism that we can make a difference even for our most behaviorally challenged children.

This book offers a strong research base for the practices recommended, but a reading of this research does not entirely convey the peacefulness that one experiences in classrooms that employ these practices. I recently had the pleasure of being in such a classroom.

The mutual care and respect that the teacher and the children in this classroom had for one another was palpable. Instruction was carefully designed to be engaging for children, and children were offered many opportunities for choice and autonomy. The classroom wasn't a silent vacuum of compliance but hummed as children went about their work, with very little need for direction or redirection. Children were self-managing: sharing the markers, offering one another feedback on their writing, and handling turn taking with ease. Yet I knew that their comfort with these behaviors was the product of much work. Their teacher had demonstrated and reinforced self-management strategies and appropriate social behaviors skillfully and consistently from day one of the school year. Gianna and Brook gave us a model and tools to create the same positive, productive environment for our students and for ourselves. My hope is that every teacher my son has will enact Gianna and Brook's vision.

REFERENCES

Akin-Little, K. A., T. L. Eckert, B. J. Lovett, and S. G. Little. 2004. "Extrinsic Reinforcement in the Classroom: Bribery or Best Practice." *School Psychology Review* 33: 344–62.

Allman, K. L., and J. R. State. 2011. "School Discipline in Public Education: A Brief Review of Current Practices." *International Journal of Educational Leadership Preparation* 6: 1–8.

Bambara, L. M., and T. P. Knoster. 2009. *Designing Positive Behavior Support Plans,* 2d ed. Washington, DC: American Association on Intellectual and Developmental Disabilities.

Battistich, V., E. Schaps, and N. Wilson. 2004. "Effects of an Elementary School Intervention on Students' 'Connectedness' to School and Social Adjustment During Middle School." *The Journal of Primary Prevention* 24: 243–62.

Birch, S. H., and G. W. Ladd. 1997. "The Teacher-Child Relationship and Children's Early School Adjustment." *Journal of School Psychology* 35: 61–79.

Bohn, C. M., A. D. Roehrig, and M. Pressley. 2004. "The First Days of School in the Classrooms of Two More Effective and Four Less Effective Primary-Grades Teachers." *The Elementary School Journal* 104: 269–87.

Brady, K., M. B. Forton, D. Porter, and C. Wood. 2003. *Rules in School.* Turners Falls, MA: Northeast Foundation for Children.

Brown, J. L., T. Roderick, L. Lantieri, and J. L. Aber. 2004. "The Resolving Conflict Creatively Program: A School-Based Social and Emotional Learning Program." In *Building Academic Success on Social and Emotional Learning,* edited by J. E. Zins, R. P. Weissberg, M. C. Wang, and H. J. Walberg. New York: Teachers College Press.

Bullara, D. T. 1993. "Classroom Management Strategies to Reduce Racially-Biased Treatment of Students." *Journal of Educational and Psychological Consultation* 4: 357–68.

Caprara, G. V., C. Barbaranelli, C. Pastorelli, A. Bandura, and P. G. Zimbardo. 2000. "Prosocial Foundations of Children's Academic Achievement." *Psychological Science* 11: 302–306.

Carter, K., and W. Doyle. 2006. "Classroom Management in Early Childhood and Elementary Classrooms." In *Handbook of Classroom Management: Research, Practice, and Contemporary Issues,* edited by C. M. Evertson and C. S. Weinstein, 373–406. New York: Routledge.

Chalk, K., and L. A. Bizo. 2004. "Specific Praise Improves On-Task Behavior and Numeracy Enjoyment: A Study of Year Four Pupils Engaged in the Numeracy Hour." *Educational Psychology in Practice* 20: 335–51.

Chin, J. K., E. Dowdy, S. R. Jimerson, and W. J. Rime. 2012. "Alternatives to Suspension: Rationale and Recommendations." *Journal of School Violence* 11: 156–73.

Conroy, M. A., and W. H. Brown. 2004. "Early Identification, Prevention, and Early Intervention with Young Children at Risk for Emotional and Behavioral Disorders: Issues, Trends, and a Call for Action." *Behavioral Disorders* 29: 224–36.

Coolahan, K., J. Fantuzzo, J. Mendez, and P. McDermott. 2000. "Preschool Peer Interactions and Readiness to Learn: Relationships Between Classroom Peer Play and Learning Behaviors and Conduct." *Journal of Educational Psychology* 92: 458–65.

Cornelius-White, J. 2007. "Learner-Centered Teacher–Student Relationships Are Effective: A Meta-Analysis." *Review of Educational Research* 77: 113–43.

Decker, D. M., D. P. Dona, and S. L. Christenson. 2007. "Behaviorally At-Risk African American Students: The Importance of Student-Teacher Relationships for Student Outcomes." *Journal of School Psychology* 45: 83–109.

Doyle, W. 2006. "Ecological Approaches to Classroom Management." In *Handbook of Classroom Management: Research, Practice, and Contemporary Issues*, edited by C. M. Evertson and C. S. Weinstein, 97–126. New York: Routledge.

Durlak, J. A., R. P. Weissberg, A. B. Dymnicki, R. D. Taylor, and K. B. Schellinger. 2011. "The Impact of Enhancing Students' Social and Emotional Learning: A Meta-Analysis of School-Based Universal Interventions." *Child Development* 82 (1): 405–32.

Elias, M. J., and N. M. Haynes. 2008. "Social Competence, Social Support, and Academic Achievement in Minority, Low-Income, Urban Elementary School Children." *School Psychology Quarterly* 23: 474–95.

Elias, M. J., and Y. Schwab. 2006. "From Compliance to Responsibility: Social and Emotional Learning and Classroom Management." In *Handbook of Classroom Management: Research, Practice, and Contemporary Issues*, edited by C. M. Evertson and C. S. Weinstein, 309–42. New York: Routledge.

Emmer, E. T., C. M. Evertson, and L. M. Anderson. 1980. "Effective Classroom Management at the Beginning of the School Year." *The Elementary School Journal* 80 (5): 219–31.

Epstein, M., M. Atkins, D. Cullinan, K. Kutash, and R. Weaver. 2008. *Reducing Behavior Problems in the Elementary School Classroom: A Practice Guide* (NCEE #2008-012). Washington, DC: National Center for Education Evaluation and Regional Assistance, Institute of Education Sciences, U.S. Department of Education. Retrieved from http://ies.ed.gov/ncee/wwc/PracticeGuide.aspx?sid=4.

Freiberg, H. J., and J. M. Lapointe. 2006. "Research-Based Programs for Preventing and Solving Discipline Problems." In *Handbook of Classroom Management: Research, Practice, and Contemporary Issues*, edited by C. M. Evertson and C. S. Weinstein, 735–86. New York: Routledge.

Gay, G. 2006. "Connections Between Classroom Management and Culturally Responsive Teaching." In *Handbook of Classroom Management: Research, Practice, and Contemporary Issues*, edited by C. M. Evertson and C. S. Weinstein, 343–70. New York: Routledge.

Gettinger, M., and K. K. Kohler. 2006. "Process-Outcome Approaches to Classroom Management and Effective Teaching." In *Handbook of Classroom Management: Research, Practice, and Contemporary Issues*, edited by C. M. Evertson and C. S. Weinstein, 73–96. New York: Routledge.

Graziano, P. A., R. D. Reavis, S. P. Keane, and S. D. Calkins. 2007. "The Role of Emotion Regulation in Children's Early Academic Success." *Journal of School Psychology* 45: 3–19.

Gregory, A., and R. S. Weinstein. 2008. "The Discipline Gap and African Americans: Defiance or Cooperation in the High School Classroom." *Journal of School Psychology* 46: 455–75.

Hamre, B. K., and R. C. Pianta. 2001. "Early Teacher-Child Relationships and the Trajectory of Children's School Outcomes Through Eighth Grade." *Child Development* 72: 625–38.

Hanh, Thich Nhat. 1991. *Peace Is Every Step: The Path of Mindfulness in Everyday Life*. New York: Bantam Books.

Harris, K. R. 1985. "Definitional, Parametric, and Procedural Considerations in Timeout Interventions and Research." *Exceptional Children* 51: 279–88.

Hemphill, S., and J. Hargreaves. 2009. "The Impact of School Suspensions: A Student Wellbeing Issue." *ACHPER Healthy Lifestyles Journal* 56: 5–11.

Hester, P. P., J. M. Hendrickson, and R. A. Gable. 2009. "Forty Years Later— The Value of Praise, Ignoring, and Rules for Preschoolers at Risk for Behavior Disorders." *Education and Treatment of Children* 32: 513–35.

Hoff, E. 2013. "Interpreting the Early Language Trajectories of Children from Low-SES and Language Minority Homes: Implications for Closing Achievement Gaps." *Developmental Psychology* 49: 4–14.

Hojnoski, R. L., K. L. Gischlar, and K. N. Missall. 2009. "Improving Child Outcomes with Data-Based Decision Making: Collecting Data." *Young Exceptional Children* 12: 32–44.

Hughes, J. N., K. A. Gleason, and D. Zhang. 2005. "Relationship Influences on Teachers' Perceptions of Academic Competence in Academically At-Risk Minority and Majority First Grade Students." *Journal of School Psychology* 43: 303–20.

Hughes, J. N., W. Lou, O. M. Kwok, and L. K. Loyd. 2008. "Teacher–Student Support, Effortful Engagement, and Achievement: A 3-Year Longitudinal Study." *Journal of Educational Psychology* 100: 1–14.

Johnson, Angela. 1995. *Humming Whispers*. New York: Scholastic.

Johnson, D. W., and R. T. Johnson. 2004. "The Three C's of Promoting Social and Emotional Learning." In *Building Academic Success on Social and Emotional Learning*, edited by J. E. Zins, R. P. Weissberg, M. C. Wang, and H. J. Walberg, 40–58. New York: Teachers College Press.

Jolivette, K. and E. A. Steed. 2010. "Classroom Management Strategies for Young Children with Challenging Behavior Within Early Childhood Settings." *NHSA Dialog* 13: 198–213.

Jones, S. M., and S. M. Bouffard. 2012. *Social and Emotional Learning in Schools from Programs to Strategies*. SRCD Policy Policy Report, 26 (4). Retrieved from www.ncflb.com/wp-content/uploads/2013/02/Social-and-Emotional-Learning-in -Schools-From-Programs-to-Strategies.pdf.

Justice, L. M., E. A. Cottone, A. Mashburn, and S. E. Rimm-Kaufman. 2008. "Relationships Between Teachers and Preschoolers Who Are at Risk: Contribution of Children's Language Skills, Temperamentally-Based Attributes, and Gender." *Early Education and Development* 19: 600–21.

Kamps, D., T. Kravits, J. Stolze, and B. Swaggart. 1999. "Prevention Strategies for At-Risk Students and Students with EBD in Urban Elementary Schools." *Journal of Emotional and Behavioral Disorders* 7: 178–88.

Katz, S. R. 1999. "Teaching in Tensions: Latino Immigrant Youth, Their Teachers, and the Structures of Schooling." *Teachers College Record* 100: 809–40.

Kern, L., L. Bambara, and J. Fogt. 2002. "Class-Wide Curricular Modification to Improve the Behavior of Students with Emotional or Behavioral Disorders." *Behavioral Disorders* 27: 317–26.

Kern, L., and N. H. Clemens. 2007. "Antecedent Strategies to Promote Appropriate Classroom Behavior." *Psychology in the Schools* 44: 65–75.

Kounin, Jacob. 1970. *Discipline and Group Management in Classrooms*. New York: Holt, Rinehart, and Winston.

Ladd, G. W., S. H. Birch, and E. S. Buhs. 1999. "Children's Social and Scholastic Lives in Kindergarten: Related Spheres of Influence?" *Child Development* 70: 1373–400.

Landrum, T. J., and J. M. Kauffman. 2006. "Behavioral Approaches to Classroom Management." In *Handbook of Classroom Management: Research, Practice, and Contemporary Issues*, edited by C. M. Evertson and C. S. Weinstein, 47–72. New York: Routledge.

Lane, K. L., J. L. Weisenbach, M. A. Little, A. Phillips, and J. Wehby. 2006. "Illustrations of Function-Based Interventions Implemented by General Education Teachers: Building Capacity at the School Site." *Education and Treatment of Children* 29: 549–71.

Larsen, R. A. A., S. B. Wanless, and S. E. Rimm-Kaufman. Manuscript under revision. "Direct and Indirect Effects of Principal Leadership on Teacher Quality and Mathematics Achievement in the Context of the *Responsive Classroom* Approach."

Leinhardt, G., C. Weidman, and K. M. Hammond. 1987. "Introduction and Integration of Classroom Routines by Expert Teachers." *Curriculum Inquiry* 17: 135–76.

Lewis, T. J., G. Sugai, and G. Colvin. 1998. "Reducing Problem Behavior Through a School-Wide System of Effective Behavioral Support: Investigation of a School-Wide Social Skills Training Program and Contextual Interventions." *School Psychology Review* 27: 446–59.

Mahar, M. T., S. K. Murphy, D. A. Rowe, J. Golden, A. T. Shields, and T. D. Raedeke. 2006. "Effects of a Classroom-Based Program on Physical Activity and On-Task Behavior." *Medicine & Science in Sports & Exercise* 38: 2086–94.

Mantzicopoulos, P. 2005. "Conflictual Relationships Between Kindergarten Children and Their Teachers: Associations with Child and Classroom Context Variables." *Journal of School Psychology* 43: 425–42.

Matheson, A. S., and M. D. Shiver. 2005. "Training Teachers to Give Effective Commands: Effects on Student Compliance and Academic Behaviors." *School Psychology Review* 34: 202–19.

Maslow, Abraham. 1966. *The Psychology of Science*. New York: Harper & Row.

Mayer, G. R. 1995. "Preventing Antisocial Behavior in the Schools." *Journal of Applied Behavior Analysis* 28: 467–78.

McIntyre, E., and J. D. Turner. 2013. "Culturally Responsive Literacy Instruction." In *Handbook of Effective Literacy Instruction*, edited by B. M. Taylor and N. K. Duke, 137–61. New York: Guilford Press.

Moberly, D. A., J. L. Waddle, and R. E. Duff. 2005. "The Use of Rewards and Punishment in Early Childhood Classrooms." *Journal of Early Childhood Teacher Education* 25: 359–66.

Montague, M., and C. Rinaldi. 2001. "Classroom Dynamics and Children At-Risk: A Follow-Up." *Learning Disability Quarterly* 24: 75–83.

Morine-Dershimer, G. 2006. "Classroom Management and Classroom Discourse." In *Handbook of Classroom Management: Research, Practice, and Contemporary Issues*, edited by C. M. Evertson and C. S. Weinstein, 127–56. New York: Routledge.

NCCP. 2013. "Basic Facts About Low-Income Children." Retrieved from www .nccp.org/publications/pub_1074.html.

Normandeau, S., and F. Guay. 1998. "Preschool Behavior and First-Grade School Achievement: The Meditational Role of Cognitive Self-Control." *Journal of Educational Psychology* 90: 111–21.

O'Connor, E., and K. McCartney. 2006. "Testing Associations Between Young Children's Relationships with Mothers and Teachers." *Journal of Educational Psychology* 98: 87–98.

Ortega y Gasset, José. 1958. *Man and Crisis*. New York: W. W. Norton.

Patrick, H., J. C. Turner, D. K. Meyer, and C. Midgley. 2003. "How Teachers Establish Psychological Environments During the First Days of School: Associations with Avoidance in Mathematics." *Teachers College Record* 105: 1521–58.

Payton, J., R. P. Weissberg, J. A. Durlak, A. B. Dymnicki, R. D. Taylor, K. B. Schellinger, and M. Pachan. 2008. *The Positive Impact of Social and Emotional Learning for Kindergarten to Eighth-Grade Students: Findings from Three Scientific Reviews*. Chicago, IL: Collaborative for Academic, Social, and Emotional Learning.

Pianta, R. C. 1999. *Enhancing Relationships Between Children and Teachers*. Washington, DC: American Psychological Association.

Pink, D. H. 2009. *Drive: The Surprising Truth About What Motivates Us*. New York: Riverhead Books.

Ponitz, C. C., S. E. Rimm-Kaufman, L. L. Brock, and L. Nathanson. 2009. "Early Adjustment, Gender Differences, and Classroom Organizational Climate in First Grade." *The Elementary School Journal* 110: 142–62.

Pontifex, M. B., B. J. Saliba, L. B. Raine, D. L. Picchietti, and C. H. Hillman. 2012. "Exercise Improves Behavioral, Neurocognitive, and Scholastic Performance in Children with Attention-Deficit/Hyperactivity Disorder." *The Journal of Pediatrics* 162 (3): 543–51.

Pressley, M., S. E. Dolezal, L. M. Raphael, L. Mohan, A. D. Roehrig, and K. Bogner. 2003. *Motivating Primary-Grade Students*. New York: Guilford Press.

Qi, C. H., and A. P. Kaiser. 2003. "Behavior Problems of Preschool Children from Low-Income Families: Review of the Literature." *Topics in Early Childhood Special Education* 23: 188–217.

Ratey, J. 2008. *Spark: The Revolutionary New Science of Exercise and the Brain*. New York: Little Brown.

Reeve, J. 2006. "Extrinsic Rewards and Inner Motivation." In *Handbook of Classroom Management: Research, Practice, and Contemporary Issues*, edited by C. M. Evertson and C. S. Weinstein, 645–64. New York: Routledge.

Rhode, G., W. R. Jenson, and D. P. Morgan. 2009. *The Tough Kid New Teacher Book: Practical Classroom Management Survival Strategies*. Eugene, OR: Pacific Northwest Publishing.

Rhode, G., W. R. Jenson, and H. K. Reavis. 1993. *The Tough Kid Book: Practical Classroom Management Strategies*. Longmont, CO: Sopris West.

Rimm-Kaufman, S. E., D. M. Early, M. J. Cox, G. Saluja, R. C. Pianta, R. H. Bradley, and C. Payne. 2002. "Early Behavioral Attributes and Teachers' Sensitivity as Predictors of Competent Behavior in the Kindergarten Classroom." *Applied Developmental Psychology* 23: 451–70.

Skinner, E. A., J. G. Wellborn, and J. P. Connell. 1990. "What It Takes to Do Well in School and Whether I've Got It: A Process Model of Perceived Control and Children's Engagement and Achievement in School." *Journal of Educational Psychology* 82: 22–32.

Solomon, D., V. Battistich, M. Watston, E. Schaps, and C. Lewis. 2000. "A Six-District Study of Educational Change: Direct and Mediated Effects of the Child Development Project." *Social Psychology of Education* 4: 3–51.

Sprick, R. 2009. *Champs: A Proactive and Positive Approach to Classroom Management.* Eugene, OR: Pacific Northwest Publishing.

Stormont, M. A., S. C. Smith, and T. J. Lewis. 2007. "Teacher Implementation of Precorrection and Praise Statements in Head Start Classrooms as a Component of a Program-Wide System of Positive Behavior Support." *Journal of Behavioral Education* 16: 280–90.

Sutherland, K. S., and J. H. Wehby. 2001. "The Effect of Self-Evaluation on Teaching Behavior in Classrooms for Students with Emotional and Behavioral Disorders." *Journal of Special Education* 35: 161–71.

Tabors, P. O. 2008. *One Child, Two Languages*, 2d ed. Baltimore: Brookes.

Thijs, J., and H. M. Koomen. 2009. "Toward a Further Understanding of Teachers' Reports of Early Teacher–Child Relationships: Examining the Roles of Behavior Appraisals and Attributions." *Early Childhood Research Quarterly* 24: 186–97.

Thompson, G. L. 2004. *Through Ebony Eyes: What Teachers Need to Know But Are Afraid to Ask About African American Students.* San Francisco, CA: Jossey-Bass.

Turner, H. S., and T. S. Watson. 1999. "Consultants' Guide to the Use of Time-Out in the Preschool and Elementary Classroom." *Psychology in the Schools* 36: 135–48.

Umbreit, J., J. B. Ferro, C. J. Liaupsin, and K. L. Lane. 2007. *Functional Behavioral Assessment and Function-Based Intervention: An Effective, Practical Approach.* Upper Saddle River, NJ: Prentice-Hall.

U.S. Department of Education. 2005. *Percentage of Public School Teacher Stayers, Movers, and Leavers Who Strongly or Somewhat Agreed with Statements About Their 2003–04 Base Year School and 2004–05 Current School.* Retrieved from http://nces.ed.gov/surveys/sass/tables/tfs_2005_04.asp.

Valiente, C., K. Lemery-Chalfant, J. Swanson, and M. Reiser. 2008. "Prediction of Children's Academic Competence from Their Effortful Control, Relationships, and Classroom Participation." *Journal of Educational Psychology* 100: 67–77.

Van Acker, R., S. H. Grant, and D. Henry. 1996. "Teacher and Student Behavior as a Function of Risk for Aggression." *Education and Treatment of Children* 19: 316–34.

Verret, C., M. C. Guay, C. Berthiaume, P. Gardiner, and L. Béliveau. 2009. "A Physical Activity Program Improves Behavior and Cognitive Functions in Children with ADHD: An Exploratory Study." *Journal of Attention Disorders* 16: 71–80.

Walker, H. M., and R. Sylwester. 1998. "Reducing Students' Refusal and Resistance." *Teaching Exceptional Children* 30: 53–58.

Watson, M., and V. Battistich. 2006. "Building and Sustaining Caring Communities." In *Handbook of Classroom Management: Research, Practice, and Contemporary Issues*, ed. C. M. Evertson and C. S. Weinstein, 253–80. New York: Routledge.

Wehlage, G. G., G. A. Rutter, G. A. Smith, N. Lesko, and R. R. Fernandez. 1989. *Reducing the Risk: Schools as Communities of Support*. New York: Falmer.

Wentzel, K. R. 1993. "Does Being Good Make the Grade? Relations Between Academic and Social Competence in Early Adolescence." *Journal of Educational Psychology* 85: 357–64.

White, K. J., K. Jones, and M. D. Sherman. 1998. "Reputation Information and Teacher Feedback: Their Influences on Children's Perceptions of Behavior Problem Peers." *Journal of Social and Clinical Psychology* 17: 11–37.

Wood, B. K., and J. B. Ferro. 2012. "An Effective Approach to Developing Function-Based Interventions in Early Childhood Classrooms." *Young Exceptional Children:* Advanced online publication. DOI: 10.1177/1096250612451760

Woolfolk Hoy, A., and C. S. Weinstein. 2006. "Student and Teacher Perspectives on Classroom Management." In *Handbook of Classroom Management: Research, Practice, and Contemporary Issues*, edited by C. M. Evertson and C. S. Weinsein, 181–219. New York: Routledge.

Wu, J. Y., J. N. Hughes, and O. M. Kwok. 2010. "Teacher–Student Relationship Quality Type in Elementary Grades: Effects on Trajectories for Achievement and Engagement." *Journal of School Psychology* 48: 357–87.